A CORPORATE CHAPLAIN'S GUIDE

Spirituality in the Workplace

Dr. Maxwell Shimba

Printed in the United States of America

SHIMBA
PUBLISHING

TABLE OF CONTENTS

Corporate Chaplains

INTRODUCTION: UNDERSTANDING THE ROLE OF CORPORATE CHAPLAINCY

By Dr. Maxwell Shimba

In the hustle and bustle of today's corporate world, employees often find themselves balancing a multitude of responsibilities, both personal and professional. Amidst the constant push for productivity and performance, there is an emerging recognition of the importance of holistic well-being. This is where corporate chaplaincy steps in—a field that not only addresses the spiritual needs of employees but also promotes a more supportive and compassionate work environment.

What is Corporate Chaplaincy?

Corporate chaplaincy involves providing spiritual care and support within the workplace. Unlike traditional roles confined to religious institutions, corporate chaplains operate within the corporate world, offering a unique blend of spiritual guidance and professional support. This role acknowledges that employees are not just workers but individuals with spiritual and emotional needs that, when addressed, can lead to a more harmonious and productive workplace.

The Evolution of Corporate Chaplaincy

The concept of integrating spirituality into the workplace is not entirely new. For centuries, various cultures and organizations have recognized the value of addressing the spiritual needs of their members. However, the formalization of corporate chaplaincy as a profession is a relatively recent development, reflecting a broader understanding of employee well-being.

In the early stages, corporate chaplaincy primarily focused on providing religious support to employees. Over time, the role has evolved to encompass a broader spectrum of spiritual care, addressing diverse beliefs and needs. Today's corporate chaplain is trained to offer support across various spiritual and religious traditions, making the workplace a more inclusive and respectful environment for everyone.

The Importance of Spiritual Well-being in the Workplace

Why is spiritual well-being important in the workplace? The answer lies in understanding the holistic nature of human beings. Spiritual well-being, like physical and mental health, plays a crucial role in an individual's overall quality of life. When employees feel supported spiritually, they are more likely to experience a sense of peace, purpose, and fulfillment. This, in turn, positively impacts their productivity, engagement, and loyalty to the organization.

Numerous studies have shown that employees who feel their spiritual needs are met are less likely to experience burnout and more likely to exhibit higher levels of job satisfaction. Furthermore, a workplace that values and supports spiritual well-being can foster a sense of community and belonging, which is essential for teamwork and collaboration.

The Role of the Corporate Chaplain

As a corporate chaplain, your primary responsibility is to provide spiritual care to employees. This involves offering a listening ear, providing counsel during times of crisis, and facilitating spiritual practices that promote well-being. Your presence in the workplace serves as a constant reminder that the organization values its employees as whole individuals, not just as cogs in the corporate machine.

The role of a corporate chaplain is multifaceted. It requires a deep understanding of various spiritual traditions, strong interpersonal skills, and the ability to navigate the complexities of the corporate environment. You will be called upon to offer support during difficult times—such as personal loss or workplace conflicts—as well as to celebrate milestones and achievements.

Building a Holistic and Supportive Work Environment

A key aspect of corporate chaplaincy is fostering a supportive and inclusive work environment. This involves creating spaces where employees feel safe to express their spiritual needs and seek support. It also means advocating for policies and practices that promote work-life balance and overall well-being.

Corporate chaplains work closely with management and human resources to develop programs and initiatives that support spiritual well-being. This can include organizing mindfulness sessions, facilitating support groups, and offering resources for personal development. By integrating these practices into the fabric of the organization, chaplains help build a culture of care and compassion.

The Impact of Corporate Chaplaincy

The impact of corporate chaplaincy extends beyond individual employees to the organization as a whole. Companies that invest in the spiritual well-being of their employees often see tangible benefits, including reduced absenteeism, lower turnover rates, and improved morale. Moreover, a workplace that prioritizes spiritual well-being is better equipped to navigate challenges and adapt to change, fostering resilience and long-term success.

Conclusion

In conclusion, corporate chaplaincy represents a vital and growing field that acknowledges the importance of spiritual well-being in the workplace. As a corporate chaplain, you have the opportunity to make a meaningful difference in the lives of employees, fostering a more holistic and supportive work environment. By addressing the spiritual needs of employees, you help create a workplace where individuals can thrive both personally and professionally, contributing to the overall success and harmony of the organization.

This book aims to provide you with the knowledge, tools, and insights needed to excel in this important role. Through practical guidance, real-life examples, and thoughtful reflections, you will learn how to navigate the complexities of corporate chaplaincy and make a lasting impact on the lives of those you serve.

Welcome to the journey of integrating spirituality into the workplace. Together, we can create a more compassionate, inclusive, and supportive work environment for all.

Dr. Maxwell Shimba

DR. MAXWELL SHIMBA

CHAPTER 01

THE NEED FOR SPIRITUALITY IN THE WORKPLACE

Understanding the Modern Workplace

The Evolution of the Workplace

The workplace has undergone significant transformations over the centuries, reflecting broader societal, technological, and economic changes. Understanding this evolution helps us appreciate the complexities and challenges of today's work environment and the growing need for holistic approaches like corporate chaplaincy.

From Agrarian to Industrial Societies

In agrarian societies, work was closely tied to the rhythms of nature and the land. People worked in family units, and their labor was integral to their community's survival and well-being. Spirituality and work were often intertwined, with religious practices marking the seasons and significant agricultural events.

The Industrial Revolution brought profound changes. As factories sprang up, people moved from rural areas to urban centers, and work became more regimented and disconnected from family life. The factory system emphasized efficiency, productivity, and the division of labor, often at the expense of workers' well-being. Long hours, harsh conditions, and the separation of home and work life became the norm. During this period, the spiritual and emotional needs of workers were largely neglected.

The Rise of the Corporate Workplace

The 20th century saw the rise of the corporate workplace. As businesses grew in size and complexity, the focus shifted to organizational efficiency, management theories, and the pursuit of profit. The corporate culture of the mid-20th century was characterized by hierarchical structures, rigid schedules, and a clear separation between personal and professional lives. Employee well-being, while recognized as important, was often secondary to organizational goals.

However, the latter part of the 20th century and the early 21st century brought significant shifts. The advent of technology, globalization, and changes in societal values began to reshape the workplace. Companies started recognizing the importance of employee satisfaction and well-being, not just for ethical reasons but also for enhancing productivity and retention. This period saw the introduction of various employee support programs, including wellness initiatives, flexible work arrangements, and corporate social responsibility efforts.

The Modern Workplace: Complex and Dynamic

Today's workplace is more complex and dynamic than ever before. The rapid pace of technological advancement, the rise of the gig economy, and the increasing importance of knowledge work have created new challenges and opportunities. Employees are expected to be more adaptable, innovative, and collaborative, often working in diverse and dispersed teams.

Several key trends characterize the modern workplace:

1. Technological Integration: Technology has revolutionized how we work, enabling remote work, virtual collaboration, and access to vast amounts of information. While technology has increased efficiency and connectivity, it has also blurred the boundaries between work and personal life, leading to issues like digital burnout and constant connectivity.

2. Globalization: Businesses operate in a global marketplace, and employees often work with colleagues and

clients from different cultural and geographical backgrounds. This diversity enriches the workplace but also requires sensitivity and adaptability to different cultural norms and practices.

3. Work-Life Balance: There is a growing recognition of the importance of work-life balance. Flexible work arrangements, telecommuting, and emphasis on mental health and wellness are increasingly seen as essential for maintaining a productive and satisfied workforce.

4. Employee Engagement and Well-being: Companies are focusing more on employee engagement and well-being, understanding that a happy and healthy workforce is more productive and loyal. This includes physical health programs, mental health support, and initiatives to foster a positive work culture.

5. Diversity and Inclusion: There is a strong emphasis on creating diverse and inclusive workplaces. Companies are recognizing the value of diverse perspectives and the need to create environments where all employees feel valued and respected.

Challenges in the Modern Workplace

Despite these positive trends, the modern workplace presents several challenges that impact employee well-being and productivity:

1. Stress and Burnout: The pressure to perform, coupled with constant connectivity, has led to high levels of stress and burnout among employees. The World Health Organization (WHO) has recognized burnout as an occupational phenomenon, highlighting its impact on mental and physical health.

2. Isolation and Disconnection: Remote work, while offering flexibility, can also lead to feelings of isolation and disconnection from colleagues and the organization. Building a sense of community and belonging in a virtual environment is a significant challenge.

3. Workplace Culture: Maintaining a positive and supportive workplace culture is critical but can be challenging, especially in large and geographically dispersed organizations. Toxic workplace cultures can lead to low morale, high turnover, and reduced productivity.

4. Ethical Dilemmas and Moral Distress: Employees often face ethical dilemmas and moral distress in their work. Navigating these challenges requires support and guidance, which is where corporate chaplaincy can play a crucial role.

The Growing Importance of Spirituality

In response to these challenges, there is a growing recognition of the importance of addressing the spiritual needs of employees. Spirituality in the workplace is not about promoting a particular religion but about creating an environment where employees can find meaning, purpose, and connection in their work.

Benefits of Spiritual Well-being

1. Enhanced Well-being: Spiritual well-being contributes to overall mental and emotional health, helping employees cope with stress and build resilience.

2. Increased Engagement and Productivity: Employees who feel their spiritual needs are met are more likely to be engaged and motivated, leading to higher productivity and job satisfaction.

3. Stronger Workplace Relationships: A focus on spirituality can foster a sense of community and strengthen relationships among colleagues, promoting teamwork and collaboration.

4. Ethical Decision-Making: Spiritual well-being supports ethical decision-making, helping employees navigate moral dilemmas with integrity and compassion.

Corporate Chaplaincy: Meeting the Need

Corporate chaplaincy is uniquely positioned to address these needs by providing spiritual care and support within the workplace. Chaplains offer a listening ear, guidance during times of crisis, and support for employees from all backgrounds and beliefs. By fostering a culture of care and compassion, corporate chaplains help create a more holistic and supportive work environment.

In the following chapters, we will explore the role of the corporate chaplain in more detail, offering practical guidance on how to integrate spirituality into the workplace and support the well-being of employees. Through case studies, best practices, and personal reflections, we aim to equip you with the tools and insights needed to excel in this important and impactful role.

The Pressures and Stresses of Contemporary Work Life

In today's fast-paced and ever-evolving corporate environment, employees face numerous pressures and stresses that impact their well-being and productivity. Understanding these challenges is crucial for recognizing the need for holistic approaches, such as corporate chaplaincy, to support employees' spiritual and emotional health.

The Nature of Modern Work Pressures

The modern workplace is characterized by a myriad of factors that contribute to employee stress. These include high-performance expectations, rapid technological advancements, increased workloads, and the constant pressure to stay connected and responsive. Let's delve deeper into these aspects:

1. High Performance Expectations

Employees are often under immense pressure to meet performance targets and deadlines. This pressure is exacerbated by competitive work environments where job security and career advancement depend on continuous high performance. The constant need to excel can lead to stress, anxiety, and burnout.

2. Rapid Technological Advancements

While technology has revolutionized the workplace, it has also introduced new challenges. The need to adapt quickly to new tools, software, and systems can be overwhelming. Additionally, technology blurs the lines between work and personal life, with employees feeling the need to be available around the clock.

3. Increased Workloads

In many organizations, employees are expected to handle increased workloads with limited resources. Downsizing, budget cuts, and lean management practices often mean that fewer employees are doing more work. This can result in long hours, reduced time for breaks, and difficulty maintaining a healthy work-life balance.

4. Constant Connectivity

The expectation to be constantly connected through emails, messaging apps, and other digital platforms means that employees find it challenging to disconnect from work. This constant connectivity can lead to digital burnout, where employees feel overwhelmed and unable to mentally switch off from work-related tasks.

The Impact of Work Stress on Employees

The pressures and stresses of contemporary work life have far-reaching effects on employees' mental, emotional, and physical health. Understanding these impacts is essential for creating supportive workplace environments:

1. Mental Health Issues

Chronic stress is a significant contributor to mental health issues such as anxiety, depression, and burnout. The relentless pressure to perform and the inability to disconnect can lead to feelings of hopelessness, fatigue, and a sense of being overwhelmed.

2. Physical Health Problems

Stress also takes a toll on physical health. It can lead to issues such as headaches, hypertension, cardiovascular problems, and a weakened immune system. The lack of time for self-care, exercise, and healthy eating further exacerbates these problems.

3. Decreased Job Satisfaction and Engagement

When employees are constantly stressed, their job satisfaction and engagement levels drop. They may feel less motivated, less committed to their work, and less enthusiastic about their roles. This can lead to decreased productivity and higher turnover rates.

4. Strained Workplace Relationships

High levels of stress can strain relationships among colleagues. Irritability, lack of patience, and reduced cooperation can lead to conflicts and a toxic work environment. This not only affects individual well-being but also hampers team dynamics and overall organizational performance.

Addressing Work Stress Through Corporate Chaplaincy

Corporate chaplaincy offers a unique and effective approach to addressing the pressures and stresses of contemporary work life. By providing spiritual and emotional support, chaplains can help employees navigate these challenges more effectively.

1. Providing a Safe Space

Corporate chaplains offer a safe and confidential space for employees to express their concerns, fears, and stresses. This non-judgmental environment allows employees to talk openly about their challenges and receive compassionate support.

2. Offering Emotional and Spiritual Guidance

Chaplains are trained to provide emotional and spiritual guidance, helping employees find meaning and purpose amidst their work pressures. This can involve counseling, prayer, meditation, and other spiritual practices tailored to individual needs.

3. Promoting Work-Life Balance

Chaplains can advocate for practices that promote a healthy work-life balance. This includes encouraging employees to take regular breaks, set boundaries between work and personal life, and engage in activities that nourish their well-being.

4. Facilitating Stress-Relief Programs

Corporate chaplains can organize stress-relief programs such as mindfulness workshops, yoga sessions, and relaxation techniques. These programs provide employees with practical tools to manage stress and enhance their overall well-being.

5. Fostering a Supportive Work Environment

By promoting a culture of care and compassion, corporate chaplains help create a supportive work environment. This involves encouraging open communication, fostering teamwork, and building a sense of community within the organization.

Conclusion

The pressures and stresses of contemporary work life are significant and multifaceted, impacting employees' mental, emotional, and physical health. Recognizing and addressing these challenges is crucial for creating a supportive and productive workplace. Corporate chaplaincy offers a holistic approach to supporting employees' well-being, providing the spiritual and emotional care needed to navigate the complexities of modern work life.

As we move forward in this book, we will explore practical strategies and insights for integrating corporate chaplaincy into the workplace. By understanding the unique role of chaplains and the benefits they bring, organizations can create environments where employees feel valued, supported, and empowered to thrive both personally and professionally.

The Gap Between Professional and Personal Life

In the modern workplace, the distinction between professional and personal life has become increasingly blurred. Employees often struggle to balance their work responsibilities with personal commitments, leading to stress, burnout, and a sense of disconnection. Understanding and addressing this gap is crucial for fostering a supportive and holistic work environment. Corporate chaplaincy plays a vital role in bridging this divide, helping employees integrate their professional and personal lives more harmoniously.

Historical Context: The Separation of Work and Life

Historically, work and personal life were closely intertwined. In agrarian societies, work was a family affair, and daily life revolved around agricultural activities. The Industrial Revolution brought about a significant shift, introducing the concept of separate workspaces and rigid working hours. This separation was further entrenched in the 20th century with the rise of corporate culture, which emphasized professionalism and the clear demarcation of work and home life.

The Modern Reality: Blurred Boundaries

In today's digital age, the boundaries between professional and personal life have become increasingly blurred. Several factors contribute to this phenomenon:

1. Technological Advancements

The proliferation of digital communication tools and mobile devices has made it possible for employees to stay connected to work 24/7. Emails, instant messaging, and video conferencing allow for constant communication, making it challenging to disconnect from work even during personal time.

2. Remote and Flexible Work

While remote and flexible work arrangements offer greater autonomy and work-life balance, they also contribute to the erosion of boundaries. The home has become a workspace, and the absence of a clear physical separation between work and personal environments can lead to an "always-on" mentality.

3. Globalization

Globalization has created a more interconnected and competitive business landscape. Employees often work across different time zones, requiring them to be available at unconventional hours. This global reach adds to the difficulty of maintaining a strict separation between professional and personal life.

4. High Performance Expectations

In many organizations, there is an expectation of high performance and continuous availability. Employees feel pressured to meet demanding targets and respond promptly to work-related matters, even outside of traditional working hours.

The Impact of the Gap on Employees

The blurred boundaries between professional and personal life have profound implications for employees' well-being and productivity:

1. Increased Stress and Burnout

The inability to disconnect from work leads to chronic stress and burnout. Employees who are constantly engaged with work-related tasks have little time to rest and recharge, resulting in physical and mental exhaustion.

2. Strained Relationships

The encroachment of work into personal time can strain relationships with family and friends. Employees may miss important personal events, leading to feelings of guilt and resentment. This strain can negatively impact both personal and professional relationships.

3. Reduced Job Satisfaction

When work dominates personal life, employees may experience a decline in job satisfaction. The constant pressure and lack of balance can lead to feelings of frustration and dissatisfaction, affecting overall morale and engagement.

4. Decreased Productivity

Ironically, the constant connectivity intended to enhance productivity can have the opposite effect. Overworked and stressed employees are less productive, more prone to errors, and less creative. The lack of clear boundaries hampers their ability to perform at their best.

Addressing the Gap Through Corporate Chaplaincy

Corporate chaplaincy offers a unique approach to addressing the gap between professional and personal life. By providing spiritual and emotional support, chaplains help employees navigate the challenges of maintaining a healthy balance.

1. Promoting Work-Life Integration

Corporate chaplains advocate for work-life integration rather than rigid separation. This approach recognizes that employees are whole individuals with interconnected professional and personal lives. Chaplains encourage practices that allow for a harmonious integration of both spheres.

2. Providing Emotional Support

Chaplains offer a safe and confidential space for employees to discuss their struggles with balancing work and personal life. Through counseling and empathetic listening, chaplains help employees develop coping strategies and find solutions to their challenges.

3. Encouraging Boundaries

Chaplains play a crucial role in promoting the importance of setting healthy boundaries. They work with employees to establish clear limits on work hours and encourage practices that support mental and emotional well-being, such as regular breaks and time off.

4. Facilitating Mindfulness and Relaxation

Chaplains can introduce mindfulness and relaxation techniques to help employees manage stress and maintain a sense of balance. Practices such as meditation, deep breathing exercises, and mindfulness workshops provide employees with tools to stay centered amidst the demands of work.

5. Supporting Personal Development

Corporate chaplains support employees' personal development by encouraging activities and pursuits outside of work. This includes hobbies, community involvement, and spiritual practices that contribute to overall well-being and fulfillment.

Building a Supportive Work Environment

A supportive work environment is essential for bridging the gap between professional and personal life. Corporate chaplains collaborate with management and HR to create policies and programs that promote work-life balance and employee well-being.

1. Flexible Work Policies

Chaplains advocate for flexible work policies that accommodate employees' personal needs. This includes flexible hours, remote work options, and family-friendly policies that support employees in balancing their responsibilities.

2. Employee Assistance Programs

Chaplains can help design and implement Employee Assistance Programs (EAPs) that provide resources and support for employees facing personal and professional challenges. EAPs offer counseling, financial advice, and other services that contribute to overall well-being.

3. Creating a Culture of Care

By fostering a culture of care and compassion, chaplains help create an environment where employees feel valued and supported. This includes recognizing employees' achievements, providing opportunities for growth, and promoting a sense of community within the organization.

Conclusion

The gap between professional and personal life is a significant challenge in the modern workplace, impacting employees' well-being, productivity, and job satisfaction. Corporate chaplaincy offers a holistic approach to addressing this gap, providing the spiritual and emotional support needed to navigate the complexities of contemporary work life.

By promoting work-life integration, encouraging healthy boundaries, and supporting personal development, corporate chaplains play a vital role in fostering a more balanced and fulfilling work environment. As we continue to explore the role of corporate chaplaincy in this book, we will uncover practical strategies and insights to help organizations and employees thrive in a world where the lines between work and personal life are increasingly blurred.

The Importance of Spiritual Well-being

In the modern corporate landscape, the focus on employee well-being has broadened to include not just physical and mental health but also spiritual well-being. This holistic approach recognizes that employees are multidimensional beings whose spiritual health significantly impacts their overall quality of life and work performance. This chapter explores the definition of spirituality in the workplace, the benefits it brings to both employees and employers and real-world examples illustrating its positive impact.

Definition of Spirituality in the Workplace

Spirituality in the workplace refers to the recognition and nurturing of the inner life of employees. It involves creating an environment where individuals feel connected to a greater purpose, experience a sense of meaning and fulfillment in their work, and are encouraged to bring their whole selves to the workplace. Unlike religious practices, workplace spirituality is inclusive and respects diverse beliefs and values. It encompasses:

1. Meaning and Purpose: Helping employees find meaning and purpose in their work, aligning their roles with their personal values and beliefs.

2. Connection and Community: Fostering a sense of belonging and community within the workplace, where employees feel connected to each other and the organization.

3. Ethical and Value-driven Work: Encouraging ethical behavior and decision-making that reflects the core values of both the individuals and the organization.

Benefits of Spiritual Well-being for Employees and Employers

For Employees:

1. Enhanced Well-being and Resilience: Employees who experience spiritual well-being are better equipped to handle stress and bounce back from adversity. They often exhibit greater emotional stability and resilience.

2. Increased Job Satisfaction and Engagement: When employees find meaning and purpose in their work, they are more likely to be satisfied with their jobs and engaged in their tasks. This leads to higher levels of motivation and productivity.

3. Improved Mental Health: Spiritual well-being can contribute to better mental health by reducing anxiety, depression, and feelings of isolation. Employees who feel spiritually supported are more likely to experience a positive state of mind.

4. Stronger Interpersonal Relationships: A spiritually nurturing environment fosters empathy, compassion, and respect among colleagues, leading to stronger interpersonal relationships and a supportive workplace culture.

For Employers:

1. Enhanced Employee Performance: Employees who are spiritually well tend to be more motivated, creative, and productive. Their enhanced well-being translates into better performance and higher-quality work.

2. Reduced Turnover and Absenteeism: Organizations that prioritize spiritual well-being often see lower turnover rates and reduced absenteeism. Employees are more likely to stay with a company that values and supports their holistic well-being.

3. Positive Workplace Culture: Promoting spirituality in the workplace helps build a positive and inclusive culture. This attracts top talent and enhances the organization's reputation as a great place to work.

4. Ethical Business Practices: A focus on spirituality encourages ethical behavior and integrity in business practices. This can lead to better decision-making, stronger stakeholder relationships, and a more sustainable business model.

Case Studies and Testimonials

Case Study 1: Tech Innovators Inc.

Tech Innovators Inc., a leading technology company, implemented a spirituality program as part of its employee wellness initiative. The program included mindfulness workshops, meditation sessions, and opportunities for employees to engage in community service projects. The results were significant:

- Employee Engagement: The company saw a 25% increase in employee engagement scores within six months of implementing the program.

- Job Satisfaction: Employee surveys indicated a 30% increase in job satisfaction, with many employees citing the spirituality program as a key factor.

- Retention Rates: The company experienced a 15% reduction in employee turnover, attributed to the improved workplace culture and support for employees' holistic well-being.

Testimonial: Jane Smith, Software Engineer

"Participating in the mindfulness workshops at Tech Innovators has been transformative for me. I feel more connected to my colleagues and more aligned with the company's mission. It's not just about coding anymore; it's about being part of a community that values me as a whole person."

Case Study 2: Healthcare Heroes Hospital

Healthcare Heroes Hospital, a large healthcare provider, recognized the high levels of stress and burnout among its staff. The hospital introduced a spiritual care program, including chaplaincy services, quiet reflection spaces, and regular workshops on work-life balance and personal growth. The outcomes were remarkable:

- Stress Reduction: Surveys showed a 40% reduction in reported stress levels among staff members who regularly participated in the program.

- Patient Care: Improved well-being among employees led to higher patient satisfaction scores, as staff were more compassionate and attentive.

- Team Cohesion: The program fostered a sense of community and support among staff, leading to improved teamwork and collaboration.

Testimonial: Dr. Michael Johnson, Surgeon

"The spiritual care program at Healthcare Heroes has been a lifesaver. It's helped me manage the stress of my job and reconnect with why I chose this profession in the first place. Knowing that the hospital cares about my well-being makes all the difference."

Case Study 3: Financial Solutions Ltd.

Financial Solutions Ltd., a global financial services firm, integrated spirituality into its corporate culture by offering personal development workshops, spiritual counseling, and opportunities for employees to engage in volunteer work. The benefits were clear:

- Ethical Decision-Making: Employees reported feeling more aligned with the company's values, leading to more ethical decision-making and enhanced trust among clients.

- Increased Productivity: The focus on spiritual well-being resulted in a 20% increase in productivity, as employees felt more motivated and fulfilled.

- Positive Culture: The firm's reputation as a supportive and value-driven organization helped attract top talent and improved overall employee morale.

Testimonial: Lisa Brown, Financial Analyst

"The spirituality program at Financial Solutions has helped me find balance and purpose in my work. I feel valued and supported, which has significantly boosted my motivation and productivity. It's refreshing to work for a company that truly cares about its employees."

Conclusion

The importance of spiritual well-being in the workplace cannot be overstated. By fostering an environment where employees can connect with their inner selves, find meaning and purpose in their work, and experience a sense of community, organizations can reap significant benefits. Corporate chaplaincy plays a crucial role in promoting spiritual well-being, offering support and guidance that enhances both personal and professional lives.

As we continue to explore the role of corporate chaplaincy in this book, we will delve deeper into practical strategies for integrating spirituality into the workplace. By understanding and addressing the spiritual needs of employees, organizations can create a more holistic, supportive, and productive work environment.

CHAPTER 02

THE ROLE OF A CORPORATE CHAPLAIN

Corporate chaplaincy is a specialized field that integrates spiritual care and professional support within the workplace. As the role gains recognition and importance, it is essential to define the responsibilities and duties of a corporate chaplain clearly. This chapter provides a comprehensive overview of what it means to be a corporate chaplain, outlining the key responsibilities and duties that define this vital role.

Responsibilities and Duties of a Corporate Chaplain

1. Providing Spiritual Support

The primary responsibility of a corporate chaplain is to offer spiritual support to employees. This involves being present and available to address the spiritual and emotional needs of individuals, regardless of their religious beliefs or backgrounds. Key aspects include:

- Listening and Counseling: Offering a compassionate ear and providing guidance to employees facing personal or professional challenges. This can include one-on-one counseling sessions, crisis intervention, and ongoing support.

- Spiritual Guidance: Helping employees explore their spiritual beliefs and practices, providing resources and advice on spiritual development, and facilitating spiritual growth within the workplace.

- Prayer and Meditation: Leading prayer sessions, meditation practices, and other spiritual activities that promote well-being and inner peace.

2. Fostering a Positive Work Environment

Corporate chaplains play a crucial role in creating and maintaining a positive and supportive work environment. This involves:

- Building Trust: Establishing trust with employees by being approachable, reliable, and maintaining confidentiality. Trust is the foundation of effective chaplaincy work.

- Promoting Inclusivity: Ensuring that the workplace is inclusive and respectful of diverse spiritual beliefs and practices. This includes advocating for policies that support religious and spiritual diversity.

- Conflict Resolution: Assisting in resolving conflicts that arise in the workplace, using mediation and negotiation skills to promote understanding and harmony among employees.

3. Organizing and Leading Spiritual Programs

Corporate chaplains are responsible for organizing and leading various spiritual programs and activities within the workplace. These programs aim to support employees' spiritual well-being and foster a sense of community. Key activities include:

- Workshops and Seminars: Conducting workshops and seminars on topics such as mindfulness, stress management, and work-life balance. These sessions provide employees with practical tools to enhance their well-being.

- Support Groups: Facilitating support groups for employees dealing with specific issues such as grief, addiction, or family problems. These groups offer a safe space for sharing experiences and receiving support.

- Community Service Projects: Organizing volunteer opportunities and community service projects that allow employees to give back and engage in meaningful activities outside of work.

4. Providing Crisis Intervention

In times of crisis, corporate chaplains are essential in providing immediate and compassionate support to employees. This includes:

- Emergency Response: Being available to respond to emergencies such as accidents, illnesses, or deaths. Providing comfort and support to affected employees and their families.

- Grief Counseling: Offering grief counseling and support to employees dealing with loss, whether it be the loss of a loved one, a colleague, or a significant life change.

- Critical Incident Stress Management: Implementing strategies to help employees cope with critical incidents and traumatic events. This includes debriefing sessions and ongoing support.

5. Supporting Organizational Goals

Corporate chaplains also contribute to achieving organizational goals by promoting employee well-being and fostering a positive corporate culture. This involves:

- Enhancing Employee Engagement: Encouraging employees to engage with their work and the organization by addressing their holistic needs and promoting a sense of purpose and fulfillment.

- Reducing Turnover and Absenteeism: By supporting employees' well-being, chaplains help reduce turnover rates and absenteeism, leading to a more stable and productive workforce.

- Improving Morale and Productivity: Creating a supportive environment where employees feel valued and supported, which in turn boosts morale and productivity.

6. Collaborating with HR and Management

Corporate chaplains work closely with HR and management to develop and implement programs that support employees' spiritual and emotional well-being. This collaboration includes:

- Developing Policies: Assisting in the development of policies that promote spiritual well-being and inclusivity within the workplace.

- Providing Training: Offering training sessions for managers and HR personnel on topics such as emotional intelligence, conflict resolution, and supporting employee well-being.

- Advising Management: Serving as a trusted advisor to management on issues related to employee morale, ethical dilemmas, and workplace culture.

Conclusion

The role of a corporate chaplain is multifaceted and essential in today's workplace. By providing spiritual support, fostering a positive work environment, organizing and leading spiritual programs, offering crisis intervention, supporting organizational goals, and collaborating with HR and management, corporate chaplains play a crucial role in enhancing the well-being of employees and the overall success of the organization.

As we continue to explore the role of corporate chaplaincy in this book, we will delve into practical strategies for effectively fulfilling these responsibilities. By understanding the comprehensive nature of the corporate chaplain's role, organizations can better support their employees and create a more holistic, inclusive, and productive work environment.

Skills and Qualities of an Effective Chaplain

The effectiveness of a corporate chaplain is largely determined by a combination of skills and personal qualities that enable them to provide meaningful spiritual and emotional support in the workplace. This chapter outlines the essential skills and qualities that define an effective chaplain, providing a comprehensive guide for those aspiring to excel in this vital role.

1. Empathy and Compassion

Definition and Importance

Empathy and compassion are the cornerstones of effective chaplaincy. Empathy involves understanding and sharing the feelings of others, while compassion goes a step further, involving a genuine desire to alleviate suffering.

Application in Chaplaincy

- Active Listening: Empathy allows chaplains to listen actively and attentively, providing a safe space for employees to express their concerns and emotions.

- Emotional Support: Compassion drives chaplains to offer comfort and support, helping employees navigate personal and professional challenges with care and understanding.

2. Strong Communication Skills

Definition and Importance

Strong communication skills are essential for conveying support, guidance, and information effectively. This includes both verbal and non-verbal communication.

Application in Chaplaincy

- Clear and Effective Communication: Chaplains must articulate their thoughts clearly and provide guidance in a manner that is easily understood.

- Non-Verbal Communication: Body language, facial expressions, and tone of voice play a significant role in building trust and conveying empathy.

3. Confidentiality and Trustworthiness

Definition and Importance

Maintaining confidentiality is crucial for building trust and ensuring that employees feel safe sharing sensitive information.

Application in Chaplaincy

- Confidential Counseling: Chaplains must handle all interactions with discretion, ensuring that personal information is kept private.

- Building Trust: Trustworthiness is essential for creating an environment where employees feel comfortable seeking support.

4. Interpersonal Skills

Definition and Importance

Interpersonal skills involve the ability to interact effectively and harmoniously with others. This includes building relationships, resolving conflicts, and collaborating with diverse groups.

Application in Chaplaincy

- Relationship Building: Chaplains must establish strong, positive relationships with employees, management, and HR.

- Conflict Resolution: Effective chaplains mediate conflicts and facilitate understanding among employees, promoting a harmonious work environment.

5. Cultural and Religious Sensitivity

Definition and Importance

Cultural and religious sensitivity involves understanding and respecting diverse beliefs, practices, and backgrounds.

Application in Chaplaincy

- Inclusivity: Chaplains must create an inclusive environment that respects and honors the spiritual and cultural diversity of the workplace.

- Tailored Support: Providing support that is sensitive to the unique needs and beliefs of each individual.

6. Problem-solving and Critical Thinking

Definition and Importance

Problem-solving and critical thinking skills enable chaplains to navigate complex situations and provide effective solutions and guidance.

Application in Chaplaincy

- Crisis Management: Chaplains must assess situations quickly and provide appropriate interventions during crises.

- Ethical Decision-Making: Applying critical thinking to navigate ethical dilemmas and make decisions that align with both organizational values and individual well-being.

7. Patience and Resilience

Definition and Importance

Patience and resilience are essential for managing the demands of chaplaincy, which often involve high-stress situations and long-term support.

Application in Chaplaincy

- Endurance: Chaplains must remain patient and composed, even in challenging circumstances.

- Self-Care: Resilience involves taking care of one's own well-being to continue providing effective support to others.

8. Organizational and Leadership Skills

Definition and Importance

Organizational and leadership skills are necessary for managing chaplaincy programs, leading initiatives, and collaborating with organizational leaders.

Application in Chaplaincy

- Program Management: Organizing workshops, seminars, and support groups effectively.

- Leadership: Leading by example and inspiring others to contribute to a positive and supportive workplace culture.

9. Ethical Integrity

Definition and Importance

Ethical integrity involves adhering to moral principles and professional standards, and ensuring that actions are guided by honesty, fairness, and respect.

Application in Chaplaincy

- Maintaining Standards: Upholding the ethical standards of the chaplaincy profession.

- Role Modeling: Serving as a role model for ethical behavior within the organization.

10. Continuous Learning and Adaptability

Definition and Importance

Continuous learning and adaptability involve staying updated with the latest research, trends, and best practices in chaplaincy and being flexible in response to changing circumstances.

Application in Chaplaincy

- Professional Development: Engaging in ongoing education and training to enhance skills and knowledge.

- Adaptability: Being open to new approaches and adjusting strategies to meet the evolving needs of the workplace.

Conclusion

The role of a corporate chaplain is multifaceted and demands a unique combination of skills and qualities. By embodying empathy, communication, confidentiality, interpersonal skills, cultural sensitivity, problem-solving, patience, organizational skills, ethical integrity, and continuous learning, chaplains can provide effective and meaningful support in the workplace.

These skills and qualities not only enable chaplains to fulfill their responsibilities but also contribute to creating a work environment where employees feel valued, supported, and motivated. As we continue to explore the role of corporate chaplaincy in this book, we will delve into practical strategies for developing and applying these essential skills, ensuring that chaplains can make a lasting impact on the lives of those they serve.

Building Trust and Relationships

Building trust and fostering strong relationships are fundamental to the effectiveness of a corporate chaplain. Trust is the cornerstone of any supportive relationship, enabling employees to feel safe and valued. This chapter explores how corporate chaplains can establish trust with employees, create a safe and confidential environment, and employ techniques for active listening and empathy.

Establishing Trust with Employees

1. Consistency and Reliability

One of the most important factors in establishing trust is being consistent and reliable. Employees need to know that they can count on the chaplain to be there when they need support.

- Regular Presence: Being consistently available in the workplace, not just during times of crisis, helps build familiarity and trust.

- Follow-Through: Keeping promises and following through on commitments demonstrates reliability and integrity.

2. Transparency and Honesty

Transparency and honesty are crucial in building trust. Employees must feel that they can rely on the chaplain to be truthful and straightforward.

- Clear Communication: Being clear about what you can and cannot do as a chaplain helps set realistic expectations.

- Open Dialogue: Encouraging open and honest communication fosters an environment where employees feel safe to share their thoughts and feelings.

3. Respect and Non-Judgment

Respecting employees' beliefs, values, and experiences is essential for building trust. A non-judgmental approach ensures that employees feel accepted and valued.

- Cultural Sensitivity: Demonstrating respect for diverse cultural and religious backgrounds builds trust and inclusivity.

- Non-Judgmental Attitude: Listening without judgment and offering support regardless of the circumstances encourages openness and trust.

Creating a Safe and Confidential Environment

1. Ensuring Confidentiality

Confidentiality is a critical component of trust. Employees need to be assured that their conversations with the chaplain will remain private.

- Confidential Conversations: Clearly communicate that all discussions are confidential and will not be shared without explicit permission.

- Secure Records: If any records are kept, ensure they are stored securely and only accessible to authorized personnel.

2. Providing a Safe Space

Creating a physical and emotional safe space for employees is essential for effective chaplaincy.

- Private Meeting Areas: Ensure that there are private and comfortable spaces for one-on-one conversations where employees can speak freely without fear of being overheard.

- Welcoming Environment: Create an atmosphere that is welcoming, inclusive, and free from distractions.

3. Clear Boundaries

Establishing and maintaining clear boundaries is important for creating a safe and professional environment.

- Professional Boundaries: Maintain professional boundaries to ensure that relationships remain supportive and appropriate.

- Role Clarity: Be clear about your role as a chaplain and the scope of the support you can provide.

Techniques for Active Listening and Empathy

1. Active Listening

Active listening is a powerful tool for building trust and demonstrating empathy. It involves fully engaging with the speaker and showing genuine interest in their words.

- Focused Attention: Give the speaker your undivided attention, maintaining eye contact and minimizing distractions.

- Reflective Listening: Reflect back on what you have heard to show understanding and clarify any points that may be unclear. This can involve summarizing or paraphrasing the speaker's words.

2. Empathetic Responses

Empathy involves understanding and sharing the feelings of others. It is essential for creating a supportive and compassionate environment.

- Verbal Cues: Use phrases that show empathy, such as "I understand how you feel" or "That sounds really challenging."

- Non-Verbal Cues: Demonstrate empathy through non-verbal cues such as nodding, appropriate facial expressions, and body language that shows you are engaged and supportive.

3. Open-Ended Questions

Open-ended questions encourage employees to share more about their experiences and feelings, fostering deeper conversations and understanding.

- Encouraging Exploration: Ask questions that invite the speaker to explore their thoughts and feelings in more detail, such as "Can you tell me more about that?" or "How did that make you feel?"

- Avoiding Yes/No Questions: Focus on questions that cannot be answered with a simple yes or no, to encourage more expansive dialogue.

4. Validating Feelings

Validating the feelings of employees helps them feel understood and respected, which is crucial for building trust.

- Acknowledging Emotions: Recognize and acknowledge the emotions the speaker is expressing. For example, "It sounds like you're feeling really overwhelmed by this situation."

- Normalizing Experiences: Help the speaker feel that their feelings are normal and understandable, reducing any sense of isolation or abnormality.

Conclusion

Building trust and relationships is fundamental to the role of a corporate chaplain. By being consistent, transparent, and respectful, chaplains can establish trust with employees. Creating a safe and confidential environment ensures that employees feel secure in seeking support. Employing techniques for active listening and empathy fosters deeper connections and understanding.

As we continue to explore the role of corporate chaplaincy in this book, we will delve into additional strategies and practices that enhance the effectiveness of chaplaincy work. By mastering these skills and qualities, chaplains can provide meaningful and impactful support to employees, contributing to a more positive and supportive workplace environment.

CHAPTER 03

INTEGRATING SPIRITUALITY INTO THE WORKPLACE

Creating a Spiritual Culture

Integrating spirituality into the workplace involves more than just implementing programs or offering resources. It requires cultivating a culture that values and supports spiritual well-being, recognizing that employees are multidimensional beings whose spiritual needs are integral to their overall well-being. This chapter explores strategies for creating a spiritual culture within a company, ensuring that spirituality is woven into the fabric of the organization.

Understanding Spiritual Culture

A spiritual culture in the workplace is one that respects and nurtures the spiritual dimensions of employees' lives. It is an environment where individuals feel free to express their spiritual beliefs and practices, find meaning and purpose in their work, and experience a sense of community and connectedness. Creating such a culture involves intentional efforts and strategies that align with the organization's values and goals.

Strategies for Integrating Spirituality into Company Culture

1. Leadership Commitment

Definition and Importance

Leadership plays a crucial role in shaping the culture of an organization. For spirituality to be effectively integrated into the workplace, it requires the commitment and support of top management.

Application

- Leading by Example: Leaders should model the behaviors and values they wish to see in the organization. This includes demonstrating respect for spiritual diversity and engaging in practices that promote spiritual well-being.

- Communicating Values: Clearly articulate the importance of spirituality and well-being in company communications, mission statements, and organizational goals.

- Allocating Resources: Dedicate resources, both financial and human, to support spiritual programs and initiatives within the workplace.

2. Inclusive Policies and Practices

Definition and Importance

Inclusive policies and practices ensure that the workplace is respectful and supportive of diverse spiritual beliefs and practices. This fosters a sense of belonging and acceptance among employees.

Application

- Flexible Scheduling: Implement policies that allow for flexible scheduling to accommodate religious practices and observances.

- Religious Accommodations: Provide spaces for prayer, meditation, or quiet reflection. Ensure that dietary needs related to religious beliefs are respected and accommodated.

- Diversity Training: Offer training programs that educate employees about different spiritual and religious traditions, promoting understanding and respect.

3. Spiritual Programs and Initiatives

Definition and Importance

Organizing programs and initiatives that support spiritual well-being can significantly enhance the spiritual culture of the workplace. These activities provide employees with opportunities to engage in spiritual practices and connect with others.

Application

- Mindfulness and Meditation Sessions: Regularly scheduled mindfulness and meditation sessions can help employees manage stress and enhance their spiritual well-being.

- Spiritual Workshops and Seminars: Offer workshops and seminars on topics such as work-life balance, finding meaning in work, and spiritual growth.

- Community Service Projects: Encourage employees to participate in community service projects. This fosters a sense of purpose and connection to the broader community.

4. Creating Spaces for Spiritual Practice

Definition and Importance

Physical spaces dedicated to spiritual practice can significantly enhance the spiritual culture of the workplace. These spaces provide employees with a quiet and comfortable environment to engage in their spiritual practices.

Application

- Prayer Rooms: Designate specific rooms for prayer and meditation. Ensure these spaces are accessible, comfortable, and respectful of all religious practices.

- Quiet Zones: Create quiet zones where employees can go for reflection and relaxation, away from the noise and distractions of the workplace.

- Nature Spaces: If possible, provide access to natural environments, such as gardens or outdoor spaces, where employees can connect with nature as part of their spiritual practice.

5. Encouraging Open Dialogue

Definition and Importance

Encouraging open dialogue about spirituality fosters a culture of acceptance and understanding. It allows employees to share their spiritual beliefs and experiences, promoting a deeper sense of community.

Application

- Discussion Groups: Organize discussion groups or forums where employees can talk about spiritual topics in a respectful and inclusive manner.

- Storytelling: Encourage employees to share stories about how their spiritual beliefs and practices influence their lives and work. This can be done through newsletters, intranet platforms, or company events.

- Support Networks: Establish support networks or affinity groups for employees who share similar spiritual beliefs. These networks can provide mutual support and a sense of belonging.

6. Recognizing and Celebrating Diversity

Definition and Importance

Recognizing and celebrating the diverse spiritual beliefs and practices of employees reinforces a culture of inclusivity and respect. It demonstrates the organization's commitment to valuing each individual's spiritual identity.

Application

- Cultural Celebrations: Celebrate diverse religious and cultural holidays within the workplace. This can include hosting events, decorating common areas, and educating employees about the significance of these observances.

- Acknowledgment Programs: Acknowledge and celebrate the spiritual milestones and achievements of employees, such as religious rites of passage or community service contributions.

- Diversity Awards: Introduce awards or recognition programs that honor employees who promote spiritual diversity and inclusivity within the organization.

Measuring the Impact

Creating a spiritual culture is an ongoing process that requires regular assessment and adjustment. Measuring the impact of spiritual initiatives helps ensure that they are meeting the needs of employees and contributing to a positive workplace culture.

1. Employee Feedback

- Surveys and Questionnaires: Regularly conduct surveys to gather feedback from employees about their experiences with spiritual programs and the overall spiritual culture of the workplace.

- Focus Groups: Organize focus groups to engage employees in deeper discussions about what is working well and what could be improved.

2. Key Performance Indicators (KPIs)

- Engagement Scores: Track employee engagement scores to assess the impact of spiritual initiatives on overall job satisfaction and morale.

- Turnover and Absenteeism: Monitor turnover rates and absenteeism to determine if there are improvements correlated with the implementation of spiritual programs.

- Participation Rates: Measure the participation rates in spiritual programs and initiatives to gauge their popularity and effectiveness.

Conclusion

Integrating spirituality into the workplace is a multifaceted endeavor that requires intentional strategies and a commitment to fostering a culture of respect, inclusivity, and support. By implementing these strategies, organizations can create a spiritual culture that enhances employee well-being, promotes ethical behavior, and contributes to a positive and productive work environment.

As we continue to explore the role of corporate chaplaincy in this book, we will delve into more practical applications and case studies that illustrate the successful integration of spirituality into various organizational contexts. By understanding and embracing the spiritual dimensions of work, organizations can create environments where employees feel valued, supported, and inspired.

Programs and Initiatives to Promote Spiritual Well-being

Introduction

Integrating spirituality into the workplace is not just about acknowledging its importance but also about taking concrete steps to promote spiritual well-being among employees. Programs and initiatives designed to support spiritual health can transform the workplace into a more harmonious and productive environment. This chapter provides detailed examples of programs and initiatives that can be implemented to foster spiritual well-being.

1. Mindfulness and Meditation Programs

Definition and Importance

Mindfulness and meditation are powerful practices that enhance spiritual well-being by helping individuals stay present, reduce stress, and gain deeper self-awareness.

Implementation

- Daily Meditation Sessions: Organize short, daily meditation sessions in a quiet space within the workplace. These sessions can be guided by a professional or facilitated by an employee trained in mindfulness techniques.

- Mindfulness Workshops: Offer regular workshops that teach employees mindfulness techniques and the benefits of incorporating mindfulness into their daily routines.

- Online Resources: Provide access to online meditation and mindfulness resources, such as apps, videos, and guided meditations, allowing employees to practice at their own pace.

Case Example

At Tech Solutions Inc., a daily 15-minute meditation session is held every morning. This practice has led to noticeable improvements in employee focus and a significant reduction in reported stress levels.

2. Spiritual Counseling and Support

Definition and Importance

Providing access to spiritual counseling and support helps employees navigate personal and professional challenges with the guidance of a trained spiritual advisor or chaplain.

Implementation

- Onsite Chaplaincy Services: Employ or contract a corporate chaplain who is available for one-on-one counseling sessions. These sessions can address a variety of issues, from personal crises to work-related stress.

- Peer Support Groups: Establish peer support groups where employees can share their experiences and offer mutual support in a safe and confidential environment.

- EAP Integration: Integrate spiritual counseling into the company's Employee Assistance Program (EAP), offering a holistic approach to employee well-being.

Case Example

Healthcare Heroes Hospital has integrated spiritual counseling into its EAP, resulting in a 30% increase in employee utilization of counseling services and a corresponding improvement in overall employee morale.

3. Spiritual Development Workshops

Definition and Importance

Workshops focused on spiritual development provide employees with tools and knowledge to enhance their spiritual well-being and integrate spiritual practices into their daily lives.

Implementation

- Personal Growth Seminars: Host seminars on topics such as finding purpose in work, balancing professional and personal life, and cultivating a positive mindset.

- Guest Speakers: Invite guest speakers from various spiritual traditions to share their insights and practices, fostering an inclusive and diverse spiritual environment.

- Interactive Workshops: Offer interactive workshops that engage employees in hands-on activities, such as journaling, vision boarding, and creative expression.

Case Example

Financial Solutions Ltd. regularly hosts spiritual development workshops, which have been instrumental in helping employees discover personal and professional purpose, leading to higher job satisfaction and retention rates.

4. Community Service and Volunteer Programs

Definition and Importance

Engaging in community service and volunteer work can provide employees with a sense of purpose and connection, both of which are essential components of spiritual well-being.

Implementation

- Volunteer Days: Organize company-sponsored volunteer days where employees can participate in community service projects during work hours.

- Partnerships with Nonprofits: Establish partnerships with local nonprofits and charities, providing employees with regular opportunities to volunteer and contribute to meaningful causes.

- Recognition Programs: Recognize and reward employees who actively participate in volunteer activities, highlighting the importance of giving back to the community.

Case Example

At GlobalTech Corp, employees are encouraged to participate in monthly volunteer days. This initiative has not only strengthened the company's community ties but also boosted employee morale and team cohesion.

5. Spiritual Resource Libraries

Definition and Importance

Providing access to a variety of spiritual resources can support employees' spiritual journeys and encourage continuous learning and growth.

Implementation

- Onsite Libraries: Create a physical library stocked with books, audio recordings, and other materials on various spiritual topics and practices.

- Digital Libraries: Develop a digital resource library that employees can access online, including e-books, podcasts, and webinars.

- Book Clubs: Organize book clubs focused on spiritual literature, providing a platform for employees to discuss and explore spiritual concepts together.

Case Example

Innovate Enterprises established an onsite and digital spiritual resource library. Employees have expressed appreciation for the diverse resources available, which support their personal and spiritual development.

6. Creating Spaces for Reflection and Prayer

Definition and Importance

Dedicated spaces for reflection and prayer provide employees with a quiet and private place to engage in their spiritual practices during the workday.

Implementation

- Prayer Rooms: Designate rooms specifically for prayer and meditation, ensuring they are accessible, comfortable, and respectful of all religious practices.

- Quiet Zones: Create quiet zones or contemplation areas where employees can take a break from their work to reflect and recharge.

- Outdoor Spaces: If possible, provide access to natural environments, such as gardens or outdoor seating areas, where employees can connect with nature.

Case Example

At GreenFields Co., the creation of an outdoor meditation garden has provided employees with a serene space to relax and reflect, contributing to overall stress reduction and increased well-being.

7. Celebrating Spiritual and Cultural Diversity

Definition and Importance

Celebrating spiritual and cultural diversity fosters an inclusive workplace where employees feel valued and respected for their unique beliefs and traditions.

Implementation

- Holiday Celebrations: Recognize and celebrate various religious and cultural holidays, hosting events and educational sessions to promote understanding and respect.

- Cultural Awareness Programs: Implement programs that educate employees about different spiritual and cultural traditions, enhancing cultural competence and inclusivity.

- Employee Stories: Encourage employees to share their spiritual journeys and cultural traditions through company newsletters, intranet platforms, or events.

Case Example

Multinational Corp celebrates a variety of religious and cultural holidays throughout the year. This practice has significantly enhanced the sense of community and inclusivity within the organization.

Conclusion

Implementing programs and initiatives to promote spiritual well-being is essential for creating a supportive and holistic work environment. By offering mindfulness and meditation programs, spiritual counseling, development workshops, community service opportunities, resource libraries, reflection spaces, and celebrating diversity, organizations can significantly enhance the spiritual well-being of their employees.

These initiatives not only support individual well-being but also contribute to a more positive, inclusive, and productive workplace culture. As we continue to explore the role of corporate chaplaincy in this book, we will delve into further strategies and best practices for fostering spiritual well-being in the workplace. By embracing these approaches, organizations can create environments where employees feel valued, supported, and inspired.

Collaborating with HR and Management

To effectively integrate spirituality into the workplace, corporate chaplains must collaborate closely with Human

Resources (HR) and management. This partnership ensures that spiritual initiatives are aligned with organizational goals, policies, and culture. In this chapter, we explore strategies for successful collaboration, the benefits of such partnerships, and practical examples of how chaplains can work with HR and management to foster spiritual well-being in the workplace.

The Importance of Collaboration

Collaboration between corporate chaplains, HR, and management is crucial for several reasons:

1. Alignment with Organizational Goals: Ensuring that spiritual initiatives support and enhance the company's mission, values, and objectives.

2. Policy Development and Implementation: Creating and enforcing policies that promote spiritual well-being and respect for diversity.

3. Resource Allocation: Securing the necessary resources, including time, budget, and personnel, to implement spiritual programs effectively.

4. Employee Engagement: Enhancing employee engagement and morale through coordinated efforts that address their holistic needs.

Strategies for Effective Collaboration

1. Building Relationships with Key Stakeholders

Definition and Importance

Establishing strong relationships with key stakeholders in HR and management is essential for successful collaboration. This involves regular communication, mutual respect, and understanding each other's roles and perspectives.

Application

- Regular Meetings: Schedule regular meetings with HR and management to discuss spiritual initiatives, share updates, and address any concerns or suggestions.

- Open Communication Channels: Maintain open lines of communication through emails, phone calls, and informal check-ins to ensure ongoing dialogue and collaboration.

- Stakeholder Engagement: Involve key stakeholders in the planning and implementation of spiritual programs to gain their insights and support.

Case Example

At Bright Future Corp, the corporate chaplain holds monthly meetings with the HR team and senior management. These meetings foster collaboration, allowing for the successful integration of spiritual well-being initiatives into the company's overall wellness strategy.

2. Integrating Spirituality into HR Policies and Practices

Definition and Importance

Integrating spirituality into HR policies and practices ensures that spiritual well-being is embedded in the company's culture and operations. This creates a supportive environment where employees feel valued and respected.

Application

- Policy Development: Work with HR to develop policies that accommodate religious practices, such as flexible scheduling for religious observances and providing prayer rooms.

- Inclusion and Diversity Training: Collaborate with HR to offer training programs that promote understanding and respect for diverse spiritual beliefs and practices.

- Employee Handbooks: Ensure that the employee handbook includes information about the company's commitment to spiritual well-being and the available resources and programs.

Case Example

Tech Innovators Inc. revised its employee handbook to include policies on religious accommodations and detailed descriptions of the spiritual support services available to employees. This initiative, developed in collaboration with the corporate chaplain, has improved employee awareness and utilization of these resources.

3. Designing and Implementing Spiritual Programs

Definition and Importance

Effective collaboration with HR and management is crucial for designing and implementing spiritual programs that meet the needs of employees and align with organizational goals.

Application

- Needs Assessment: Conduct surveys and focus groups to assess employees' spiritual needs and preferences. Use this data to design relevant and impactful programs.

- Program Development: Work with HR and management to develop and roll out spiritual programs, such as mindfulness workshops, meditation sessions, and support groups.

- Ongoing Evaluation: Continuously evaluate the effectiveness of spiritual programs through employee feedback and participation rates. Make adjustments as needed to ensure their success.

Case Example

Financial Solutions Ltd. introduced a series of mindfulness workshops developed through a collaborative effort between the corporate chaplain, HR, and management.

The program's success, measured by high participation rates and positive employee feedback, highlights the importance of collaboration in program design and implementation.

4. Promoting and Communicating Spiritual Initiatives

Definition and Importance

Effective communication is key to promoting spiritual initiatives and ensuring that employees are aware of and engaged with the available programs and resources.

Application

- Internal Communications: Utilize internal communication channels, such as newsletters, intranet platforms, and bulletin boards, to promote spiritual initiatives and share success stories.

- Leadership Endorsement: Encourage leaders and managers to endorse and participate in spiritual programs, demonstrating their support and commitment.

- Employee Involvement: Involve employees in promoting spiritual initiatives by sharing their experiences and testimonials through company communication channels.

Case Example

At GlobalTech Corp, the corporate chaplain collaborated with the HR communications team to launch a monthly newsletter featuring articles on spiritual well-being, upcoming events, and employee testimonials. This approach has increased awareness and participation in spiritual programs.

5. Training and Development for Managers and HR Professionals

Definition and Importance

Providing training and development opportunities for managers and HR professionals helps them understand the importance of spiritual well-being and equips them with the skills to support employees effectively.

Application

- Workshops and Seminars: Offer workshops and seminars on topics such as emotional intelligence, active listening, and supporting employees' spiritual needs.

- Resource Materials: Develop and distribute resource materials that provide guidance on integrating spirituality into management practices and HR policies.

- Ongoing Education: Encourage continuous learning through online courses, webinars, and professional development programs focused on spiritual well-being.

Case Example

Healthcare Heroes Hospital implemented a training program for managers and HR professionals, developed in collaboration with the corporate chaplain. The program covers topics such as cultural competence, supporting spiritual diversity, and effective communication. This initiative has improved managers' ability to support their teams and foster a more inclusive workplace.

Benefits of Collaboration

1. Enhanced Employee Well-being

Collaborating with HR and management ensures that spiritual initiatives are comprehensive and well-supported, leading to enhanced employee well-being. Employees feel valued and supported, contributing to higher job satisfaction and morale.

2. Improved Organizational Culture

A collaborative approach to integrating spirituality into the workplace fosters a positive and inclusive organizational culture. This culture promotes respect, empathy, and a sense of community, which are essential for a thriving workplace.

3. Increased Engagement and Retention

hen employees feel their spiritual needs are met, they are more likely to be engaged and committed to the organization. This leads to higher retention rates and reduced turnover, benefiting the organization as a whole.

4. Alignment with Organizational Goals

Collaboration ensures that spiritual initiatives align with the organization's goals and values, enhancing overall organizational performance and success.

Conclusion

Collaboration between corporate chaplains, HR, and management is essential for successfully integrating spirituality into the workplace. By building strong relationships, integrating spirituality into HR policies and practices, designing and implementing effective programs, promoting initiatives, and providing training and development, chaplains can create a supportive environment that enhances employee well-being and organizational success.

As we continue to explore the role of corporate chaplaincy in this book, we will delve into further strategies and best practices for fostering spiritual well-being in the workplace. Through effective collaboration, organizations can create environments where employees feel valued, supported, and inspired.

Practical Tools and Resources

Integrating spirituality into the workplace involves providing employees with practical tools and resources that support their spiritual well-being. Meditation and mindfulness practices are among the most effective and accessible methods for fostering a sense of inner peace, focus, and overall well-being. This chapter explores various meditation and mindfulness practices that can be implemented in the workplace, offering practical guidance on how to introduce and sustain these practices effectively.

Meditation Practices

1. Guided Meditation

Definition and Importance

Guided meditation involves a facilitator leading participants through a series of instructions to help them relax and focus their minds. This practice is beneficial for beginners and can be tailored to address specific needs, such as stress reduction, focus, or relaxation.

Implementation

- Regular Sessions: Schedule regular guided meditation sessions, such as daily or weekly, led by a trained facilitator. These sessions can be held in a quiet room or a designated meditation space.

- Diverse Themes: Offer guided meditations with various themes, such as stress relief, gratitude, and compassion, to cater to different needs and preferences.

- Digital Access: Provide access to guided meditation recordings or apps that employees can use at their convenience.

Example Practice

"Begin by sitting comfortably with your back straight and your hands resting on your lap. Close your eyes and take a deep breath in, feeling your lungs expand. Slowly exhale, releasing any tension. Imagine a warm, golden light surrounding you, filling you with a sense of calm and peace. As you continue to breathe deeply, allow yourself to be guided by the facilitator's voice, letting go of any stress or worries."

2. Mindful Breathing

Definition and Importance

Mindful breathing is a simple yet powerful practice that involves focusing on the breath to bring attention to the present moment. It is an effective way to reduce stress and enhance concentration.

Implementation

- Breathing Exercises: Teach employees simple breathing exercises that they can practice at their desks or in a quiet space. These exercises can be included in daily routines or as part of stress management programs.

- Reminder Tools: Use reminder tools, such as posters or digital prompts, to encourage employees to practice mindful breathing throughout the day.

- Workshops: Offer workshops on mindful breathing techniques, explaining the benefits and providing hands-on practice.

Example Practice

"Find a comfortable sitting position with your feet flat on the floor. Close your eyes or soften your gaze. Take a deep breath in through your nose, counting to four. Hold your breath for a count of four. Then, slowly exhale through your mouth for a count of four. Repeat this cycle for a few minutes, focusing solely on your breath and the sensation of air entering and leaving your body."

3. Body Scan Meditation

Definition and Importance

Body scan meditation involves systematically focusing on different parts of the body, bringing awareness and relaxation to each area. This practice helps reduce physical tension and enhances mind-body connection.

Implementation

- Group Sessions: Conduct group body scan meditation sessions, led by a facilitator, in a quiet and comfortable space.

- Individual Practice: Encourage employees to practice body scan meditation individually, providing them with guided recordings or written instructions.

- Incorporation into Breaks: Integrate short body scan meditations into regular break times to help employees relax and recharge.

Example Practice

"Lie down or sit comfortably with your eyes closed. Take a deep breath and bring your attention to your feet. Notice any sensations or tension in this area. Slowly move your focus up to your ankles, calves, knees, and thighs, observing and relaxing each part. Continue this process, moving up through your body, until you reach the top of your head. Allow yourself to experience a sense of complete relaxation and awareness."

4. Loving-Kindness Meditation

Definition and Importance

Loving-kindness meditation, also known as Metta meditation, involves cultivating feelings of compassion and love towards oneself and others. This practice enhances emotional well-being and fosters a positive and empathetic work environment.

Implementation

- Group Practice: Hold group loving-kindness meditation sessions, guiding participants through the practice of sending positive intentions to themselves and others.

- Individual Practice: Provide resources for employees to practice loving-kindness meditation individually, such as guided recordings or written scripts.

- Incorporation into Meetings: Begin or end team meetings with a short loving-kindness meditation to promote a sense of unity and compassion.

Example Practice

"Sit comfortably and close your eyes. Take a few deep breaths, allowing yourself to relax. Begin by focusing on yourself, silently repeating the phrases, 'May I be happy. May I be healthy. May I be safe. May I live with ease.' After a few minutes, bring to mind someone you care about and repeat the phrases for them. Gradually extend these feelings of loving-kindness to others in your life, including colleagues, acquaintances, and even those with whom you have difficulties."

Mindfulness Practices

1. Mindful Walking

Definition and Importance

Mindful walking involves paying full attention to the experience of walking, using it as a form of moving meditation. This practice helps increase mindfulness and can be a refreshing break during the workday.

Implementation

- Mindful Walking Paths: Designate specific areas or paths within the workplace for mindful walking, such as garden paths or quiet corridors.

- Guided Sessions: Offer guided mindful walking sessions during breaks or as part of wellness programs.

- Individual Practice: Encourage employees to practice mindful walking individually, providing guidelines and tips.

Example Practice

"Begin walking at a slow and steady pace. Focus on the sensation of your feet touching the ground with each step. Notice the movement of your legs, the shift of your weight, and the rhythm of your breath. If your mind wanders, gently bring your attention back to the experience of walking. Continue for several minutes, allowing yourself to be fully present in each step."

2. Mindful Eating

Definition and Importance

Mindful eating involves paying full attention to the experience of eating, savoring each bite, and recognizing the flavors, textures, and sensations. This practice promotes a healthier relationship with food and enhances overall mindfulness.

Implementation

- Mindful Eating Breaks: Encourage employees to take mindful eating breaks, where they focus solely on their meal without distractions.

- Workshops: Offer workshops on mindful eating, teaching employees how to incorporate mindfulness into their eating habits.

- Digital Resources: Provide digital resources, such as videos or articles, on the benefits and techniques of mindful eating.

Example Practice

"During your meal, take a moment to appreciate the appearance and aroma of the food. As you take a bite, focus on the taste, texture, and sensation in your mouth. Chew slowly and thoroughly, noticing how the flavors change and develop. Put down your utensils between bites, taking time to savor each mouthful. Pay attention to the feelings of hunger and fullness, eating until you feel satisfied."

3. Mindfulness Exercises

Definition and Importance

Mindfulness exercises are simple practices that help individuals stay present and aware, reducing stress and enhancing focus. These exercises can be easily incorporated into the workday.

Implementation

- Mindfulness Minutes: Introduce short mindfulness exercises, such as one-minute breathing or five-minute body scans, that employees can practice at their desks or during breaks.

- Mindfulness Challenges: Organize mindfulness challenges, encouraging employees to practice mindfulness exercises daily for a set period.

- Digital Reminders: Use digital reminders, such as calendar notifications or mindfulness apps, to prompt employees to take mindfulness breaks.

Example Practice

"Take a moment to sit comfortably and close your eyes. Bring your attention to your breath, noticing the sensation of air entering and leaving your body. As you breathe in, silently say to yourself, 'Breathing in, I know I am breathing in.' As you breathe out, say, 'Breathing out, I know I am breathing out.' Continue this practice for one minute, focusing solely on your breath and the present moment."

Conclusion

Meditation and mindfulness practices are powerful tools for promoting spiritual well-being in the workplace. By incorporating guided meditation, mindful breathing, body scan meditation, loving-kindness meditation, mindful walking, mindful eating, and other mindfulness exercises, organizations can create a supportive environment that enhances employees' overall well-being and productivity.

These practices not only reduce stress and improve focus but also foster a sense of community and connectedness among employees. As we continue to explore the role of corporate chaplaincy in this book, we will delve into further strategies and best practices for fostering spiritual well-being in the workplace. By providing practical tools and resources, organizations can create environments where employees feel valued, supported, and inspired.

Spiritual Workshops and Seminars

Spiritual workshops and seminars are powerful tools for fostering spiritual well-being in the workplace. These events provide employees with opportunities to explore spiritual concepts, develop personal growth, and build a supportive community. This chapter discusses the importance of spiritual workshops and seminars, offers practical guidance for organizing these events, and provides examples of topics that can be covered.

The Importance of Spiritual Workshops and Seminars

Spiritual workshops and seminars offer several benefits to employees and organizations:

1. Personal Growth and Development: These events help employees explore their spirituality, leading to personal growth and a deeper sense of purpose.

2. Stress Reduction: Workshops and seminars on topics such as mindfulness and meditation can equip employees with tools to manage stress effectively.

3. Community Building: These events foster a sense of community and connection among employees, promoting a positive and supportive workplace culture.

4. Enhanced Well-being: Engaging in spiritual exploration and practices can improve overall well-being, leading to increased job satisfaction and productivity.

Organizing Spiritual Workshops and Seminars

1. Identifying Topics and Goals

Definition and Importance

Selecting relevant topics and setting clear goals are crucial for the success of spiritual workshops and seminars. Topics should align with the interests and needs of employees and support the overall goals of the organization.

Application

- Needs Assessment: Conduct surveys or focus groups to understand employees' interests and needs. Use this feedback to select topics that will resonate with them.

- Goal Setting: Define the objectives of each workshop or seminar. For example, a goal might be to teach stress management techniques or to foster a sense of community.

Example Topics

- Mindfulness and Meditation

- Finding Meaning and Purpose in Work

- Stress Management and Resilience

- Spiritual Practices for Daily Life

- Building a Compassionate Workplace

- Exploring Diverse Spiritual Traditions

2. Planning and Logistics

Definition and Importance

Effective planning and logistics are essential to ensure that spiritual workshops and seminars run smoothly and are well-attended.

Application

- Scheduling: Choose dates and times that accommodate employees' schedules. Consider offering sessions during lunch breaks or after work hours to maximize participation.

- Location: Select a comfortable and accessible location for the events. This could be a conference room, a dedicated wellness space, or even an outdoor area.

- Facilitators: Identify and invite knowledgeable and engaging facilitators to lead the workshops and seminars. These could be internal staff, external experts, or professional trainers.

Example Practice

At Wellness Tech Ltd., spiritual workshops are scheduled during extended lunch breaks, allowing employees to participate without disrupting their workday. The company uses a dedicated wellness room equipped with comfortable seating and calming decor to create a conducive environment for these sessions.

3. Promoting the Events

Definition and Importance

Promoting spiritual workshops and seminars effectively ensures that employees are aware of and excited about these opportunities.

Application

- Communication Channels: Use various communication channels to promote the events, such as emails, newsletters, intranet platforms, and bulletin boards.

- Personal Invitations: Encourage managers and leaders to personally invite their team members to attend the workshops and seminars.

- Incentives: Consider offering incentives for participation, such as certificates of completion, refreshments, or small rewards.

Example Practice

Global Enterprises uses a multi-channel approach to promote its spiritual workshops, including email announcements, posters in common areas and mentions in company-wide meetings. Additionally, employees who attend three or more workshops receive a wellness kit as a token of appreciation.

4. Facilitating the Workshops and Seminars

Definition and Importance

Facilitating spiritual workshops and seminars effectively requires creating a supportive and engaging environment where participants feel comfortable exploring and sharing.

Application

- Interactive Sessions: Design workshops and seminars to be interactive, incorporating activities such as group discussions, experiential exercises, and hands-on practices.

- Safe Space: Ensure that the environment is welcoming and non-judgmental, allowing participants to express themselves freely and respectfully.

- Feedback Mechanism: Collect feedback from participants to continuously improve future workshops and seminars. This can be done through surveys or informal discussions.

Example Practice

At Creative Minds Corp, workshops are designed to be highly interactive, with activities such as guided meditations, group reflections, and role-playing exercises. Participants consistently report feeling more engaged and connected as a result of these dynamic sessions.

Examples of Spiritual Workshop and Seminar Topics

1. Mindfulness and Meditation

Description

This workshop introduces participants to mindfulness and meditation practices that can be integrated into daily life to reduce stress and enhance focus.

Activities

- Guided meditation sessions
- Mindfulness exercises
- Group discussions on the benefits of mindfulness

2. Finding Meaning and Purpose in Work

Description

This seminar explores how employees can find deeper meaning and purpose in their work, aligning their professional roles with their personal values and goals.

Activities

- Personal reflection exercises

- Vision boarding

- Discussions on aligning work with values

3. Stress Management and Resilience

Description

This workshop provides tools and techniques for managing stress and building resilience, helping employees navigate challenges with greater ease.

Activities

- Breathing exercises and relaxation techniques

- Role-playing stress management scenarios

- Developing personal resilience plans

4. Spiritual Practices for Daily Life

Description

This seminar introduces participants to various spiritual practices that can be incorporated into daily routines to enhance overall well-being.

Activities

- Journaling exercises

- Creating personal rituals

- Sharing and discussing different spiritual practices

5. Building a Compassionate Workplace

Description

This workshop focuses on fostering compassion and empathy in the workplace, creating a more supportive and connected work environment.

Activities

- Empathy-building exercises

- Group discussions on compassion in the workplace

- Developing action plans for promoting compassion

6. Exploring Diverse Spiritual Traditions

Description

This seminar offers an opportunity to learn about and appreciate diverse spiritual traditions, promoting inclusivity and respect in the workplace.

Activities

- Presentations on different spiritual traditions

- Cultural storytelling

- Group discussions on inclusivity and respect

Conclusion

Spiritual workshops and seminars are invaluable tools for promoting spiritual well-being in the workplace. By organizing and facilitating these events, organizations can provide employees with opportunities for personal growth, stress reduction, and community building. Effective planning, promotion, and facilitation are key to the success of these initiatives.

As we continue to explore the role of corporate chaplaincy in this book, we will delve into further strategies and best practices for fostering spiritual well-being in the workplace. By providing practical tools and resources, organizations can create environments where employees feel valued, supported, and inspired.

Providing Resources for Spiritual Growth

Supporting employees' spiritual growth involves offering a variety of resources that cater to diverse spiritual needs and preferences. These resources can enhance employees' overall well-being, promote a sense of purpose, and foster a more inclusive and supportive workplace culture. This chapter explores different types of resources that can be provided to facilitate spiritual growth, offering practical guidance on how to make these resources accessible and engaging.

The Importance of Providing Resources for Spiritual Growth

1. Holistic Well-being: Spiritual resources contribute to the holistic well-being of employees, addressing not only

their professional needs but also their personal and spiritual dimensions.

2. Enhanced Engagement: Employees who feel supported in their spiritual growth are more likely to be engaged, motivated, and productive.

3. Inclusive Culture: Providing diverse spiritual resources promotes inclusivity and respect for different beliefs and practices within the workplace.

Types of Resources for Spiritual Growth

1. Spiritual Libraries

Definition and Importance

A spiritual library offers a collection of books, audio recordings, and other materials on various spiritual topics and practices. It serves as a valuable resource for employees seeking to deepen their spiritual understanding and practice.

Implementation

- Physical Library: Establish a physical library in a quiet, accessible location within the workplace. Stock it with a diverse range of materials, including books on mindfulness, meditation, religious texts, and personal development.

- Digital Library: Create a digital library accessible through the company's intranet or a dedicated platform. Include e-books, audiobooks, podcasts, and videos on spiritual topics.

- Curated Selections: Regularly update the library with new materials and curate selections based on employee interests and feedback.

Example Practice

At Harmony Corp, the spiritual library includes sections on mindfulness, different religious traditions, and self-help. Employees can borrow physical books or access digital resources through the company's intranet. This initiative has been well-received, with many employees citing it as a valuable tool for personal growth.

2. Online Resources and Apps

Definition and Importance

Providing access to online resources and mobile apps allows employees to engage in spiritual practices and learning at their convenience. These digital tools can be especially useful for remote or hybrid work environments.

Implementation

- Resource Lists: Compile and share lists of recommended websites, online courses, and mobile apps that focus on spiritual growth and well-being.

- Subscriptions: Offer company-wide subscriptions to popular meditation, mindfulness, or spiritual growth apps.

- Webinars and Online Workshops: Organize webinars and online workshops led by experts on various spiritual topics, allowing employees to participate from anywhere.

Example Practice

Tech Solutions Inc. provides access to a range of online resources, including a subscription to a leading meditation app. The company also hosts monthly webinars on topics such as stress management and finding purpose in work. These resources have become an integral part of the company's wellness program.

3. Personal Development Programs

Definition and Importance

Personal development programs that include spiritual components help employees explore and enhance their spiritual well-being. These programs can be tailored to address specific needs and interests.

Implementation

- Workshops and Seminars: Organize workshops and seminars on topics such as mindfulness, resilience, and spiritual growth. Ensure these sessions are interactive and engaging.

- Mentorship Programs: Develop mentorship programs where employees can receive guidance and support from experienced mentors on their spiritual journeys.

- Retreats and Offsite Programs: Offer opportunities for employees to attend retreats or offsite programs focused on spiritual growth and personal development.

Example Practice

Global Enterprises hosts an annual retreat focused on personal and spiritual development. The retreat includes workshops on mindfulness, group discussions, and outdoor activities. Participants consistently report feeling rejuvenated and more connected to their personal and professional goals.

4. Support Groups and Peer Networks

Definition and Importance

Support groups and peer networks provide employees with a sense of community and belonging, allowing them to share their experiences and support each other's spiritual growth.

Implementation

- Employee Resource Groups (ERGs): Establish ERGs focused on spiritual growth and well-being. These groups can meet regularly to discuss spiritual topics, share resources, and support each other.

- Discussion Forums: Create online discussion forums or social media groups where employees can connect, share insights, and discuss spiritual matters.

- Peer-Led Sessions: Encourage employees to lead sessions or workshops on spiritual practices they are passionate about, fostering a sense of ownership and community.

Example Practice

Innovative Tech Ltd. has several ERGs, including one dedicated to mindfulness and spiritual growth. The group meets bi-weekly for meditation sessions, book discussions, and peer support. This initiative has strengthened community bonds and provided valuable support for participants.

5. Spiritual Coaching and Counseling

Definition and Importance

Providing access to spiritual coaching and counseling helps employees navigate personal and professional challenges with the guidance of trained professionals.

Implementation

- Onsite Chaplaincy: Employ or contract a corporate chaplain who can provide one-on-one spiritual counseling and support to employees.

- External Referrals: Develop a network of external spiritual coaches and counselors who can offer specialized support as needed.

- Confidential Services: Ensure that coaching and counseling services are confidential and accessible, promoting trust and utilization.

Example Practice

At Wellness Tech Ltd., the corporate chaplain offers confidential one-on-one counseling sessions for employees facing personal or professional challenges. The availability of these services has led to increased employee satisfaction and well-being.

Creating a Culture of Spiritual Growth

1. Leadership Support and Engagement

Definition and Importance

Leadership support and engagement are critical for fostering a culture that values and promotes spiritual growth.

Implementation

- Lead by Example: Encourage leaders to participate in and support spiritual growth initiatives, demonstrating their commitment to employee well-being.

- Communication: Regularly communicate the importance of spiritual growth and the available resources through company newsletters, meetings, and internal platforms.

Example Practice

At Creative Minds Corp, senior leaders actively participate in spiritual workshops and promote the importance of spiritual well-being in company communications. This leadership engagement has significantly boosted employee participation and support for these initiatives.

2. Employee Involvement and Feedback

Definition and Importance

Involving employees in the development and evaluation of spiritual growth resources ensures that these initiatives meet their needs and preferences.

Implementation

- Feedback Mechanisms: Use surveys, focus groups, and suggestion boxes to gather employee feedback on spiritual growth resources and programs.

- Inclusive Planning: Involve employees in the planning and implementation of spiritual growth initiatives, allowing them to take ownership and contribute ideas.

Example Practice

Financial Solutions Ltd. regularly surveys employees to gather feedback on their spiritual growth programs. This feedback is used to refine and enhance the offerings, ensuring they remain relevant and impactful.

3. Continuous Improvement and Innovation

Definition and Importance

Continuously improving and innovating spiritual growth resources keeps them relevant and effective, adapting to changing employee needs and preferences.

Implementation

- Regular Reviews: Conduct regular reviews of spiritual growth programs and resources to identify areas for improvement and innovation.

- Pilot Programs: Test new ideas and approaches through pilot programs, gathering feedback and making adjustments before full implementation.

Example Practice

At Harmony Corp, the spiritual growth programs are reviewed annually, and new initiatives are piloted regularly. This commitment to continuous improvement ensures that the offerings remain fresh and engaging for employees.

Conclusion

Providing resources for spiritual growth is a vital component of fostering a supportive and inclusive workplace culture. By offering spiritual libraries, online resources, personal development programs, support groups, and spiritual coaching, organizations can support employees' holistic well-being and enhance overall engagement and productivity.

As we continue to explore the role of corporate chaplaincy in this book, we will delve into further strategies and best practices for fostering spiritual well-being in the workplace. By providing practical tools and resources, organizations can create environments where employees feel valued, supported, and inspired.

CHAPTER 04

ADDRESSING EMPLOYEE NEEDS

Common Issues Faced by Employees

Stress, Burnout, and Work-Life Balance

Introduction

In today's fast-paced work environment, employees often face significant challenges related to stress, burnout, and work-life balance. These issues can negatively impact their well-being, productivity, and overall job satisfaction. This chapter explores the common issues faced by employees, focusing on stress, burnout, and work-life balance, and offers practical strategies for addressing these challenges through corporate chaplaincy.

Understanding Stress in the Workplace

Definition and Importance

Stress is the body's natural response to demanding situations. While some stress can be motivating, excessive and chronic stress can lead to serious health issues, both physical and mental. Understanding the sources and effects of workplace stress is essential for creating effective interventions.

Sources of Workplace Stress

1. High Workloads: Excessive workloads and unrealistic deadlines can overwhelm employees, leading to chronic stress.

2. Lack of Control: Feeling a lack of control over work tasks or decisions can increase stress levels.

3. Unclear Expectations: Unclear job expectations and inconsistent feedback can cause anxiety and stress.

4. Poor Work Relationships: Conflict with colleagues or managers can create a stressful work environment.

5. Work-Life Imbalance: Difficulty balancing work responsibilities with personal life can exacerbate stress.

Effects of Chronic Stress

1. Physical Health Issues: Chronic stress can lead to headaches, hypertension, cardiovascular problems, and a weakened immune system.

2. Mental Health Issues: Prolonged stress can contribute to anxiety, depression, and burnout.

3. Reduced Productivity: High-stress levels can impair cognitive functions, leading to decreased productivity and performance.

4. Increased Absenteeism: Stress-related health issues often result in higher absenteeism and presenteeism rates.

Addressing Stress Through Corporate Chaplaincy

1. Providing Stress Management Resources

Definition and Importance

Offering resources and tools to manage stress can help employees cope more effectively with workplace pressures.

Implementation

- Workshops and Seminars: Organize workshops on stress management techniques, such as mindfulness, time management, and relaxation exercises.

- Resource Materials: Provide access to articles, books, and online resources focused on stress reduction strategies.

- Mindfulness Programs: Implement mindfulness and meditation programs to help employees develop coping mechanisms.

Example Practice

At Wellness Tech Ltd., regular stress management workshops are conducted by the corporate chaplain, covering topics such as mindfulness, breathing exercises, and effective time management. These workshops have significantly reduced reported stress levels among employees.

2. Offering Counseling and Support

Definition and Importance

Providing access to counseling and support services helps employees address stress-related issues in a confidential and supportive environment.

Implementation

- One-on-One Counseling: Offer confidential counseling sessions with a corporate chaplain or trained counselor.

- Peer Support Groups: Establish peer support groups where employees can share their experiences and coping strategies.

- Employee Assistance Programs (EAPs): Integrate spiritual counseling into the company's EAP to provide holistic support.

Example Practice

At Harmony Corp, the corporate chaplain provides one-on-one counseling sessions for employees experiencing high levels of stress. This service has been well-received and has helped many employees manage their stress more effectively.

Understanding Burnout

Definition and Importance

Burnout is a state of emotional, physical, and mental exhaustion caused by prolonged and excessive stress. It occurs when employees feel overwhelmed, emotionally drained, and unable to meet constant demands. Recognizing and addressing burnout is crucial for maintaining a healthy and productive workforce.

Signs of Burnout

1. Exhaustion: Persistent fatigue and lack of energy.

2. Detachment: Feeling disconnected from work and colleagues.

3. Reduced Performance: Decreased productivity and sense of accomplishment.

4. Negative Attitudes: Cynicism and negativity towards work and colleagues.

Causes of Burnout

1. Excessive Workloads: Consistently high demands and long hours.

2. Lack of Support: Insufficient support from management or colleagues.

3. Poor Work-Life Balance: Inability to separate work from personal life.

4. Lack of Autonomy: Feeling powerless to influence decisions affecting one's job.

Addressing Burnout Through Corporate Chaplaincy

1. Promoting Work-Life Balance

Definition and Importance

Encouraging a healthy work-life balance helps prevent burnout and promotes overall well-being.

Implementation

- Flexible Work Arrangements: Offer flexible working hours, remote work options, and compressed workweeks to help employees balance their personal and professional lives.

- Encouraging Time Off: Promote the use of vacation days and personal time off. Encourage employees to take regular breaks and avoid overworking.

- Work-Life Balance Programs: Develop programs and initiatives that support work-life balance, such as wellness days, family-friendly policies, and time management workshops.

Example Practice

Global Enterprises has implemented a flexible work policy that allows employees to choose their working hours and work from home when needed. This initiative, supported by the corporate chaplain, has helped improve work-life balance and reduce burnout.

2. Providing Emotional and Spiritual Support

Definition and Importance

Offering emotional and spiritual support helps employees cope with the demands of their job and prevents burnout.

Implementation

- Regular Check-Ins: Conduct regular check-ins with employees to discuss their well-being and provide support.

- Spiritual Counseling: Offer spiritual counseling sessions to help employees find meaning and purpose in their work.

- Supportive Community: Foster a supportive workplace community where employees feel valued and connected.

Example Practice

At Creative Minds Corp, the corporate chaplain conducts monthly check-ins with employees to discuss their well-being and offer support. These sessions have been instrumental in preventing burnout and promoting a positive work environment.

Work-Life Balance

Definition and Importance

Achieving a healthy work-life balance involves managing work responsibilities alongside personal life, ensuring neither aspect is neglected. This balance is essential for maintaining overall well-being and productivity.

Challenges to Work-Life Balance

1. Long Working Hours: Extended work hours can encroach on personal time, leading to stress and burnout.

2. Constant Connectivity: The expectation to be always available, even outside of work hours, can disrupt personal life.

3. High Job Demands: Intense job demands can make it difficult to allocate time for personal activities and relationships.

4. Lack of Boundaries: Blurred boundaries between work and personal life can lead to an imbalance.

Strategies for Promoting Work-Life Balance

1. Encouraging Boundary Setting

Definition and Importance

Setting clear boundaries between work and personal life is crucial for maintaining a healthy balance.

Implementation

- Clear Policies: Establish policies that discourage work-related communication outside of regular working hours.

- Boundary Training: Offer training on setting and maintaining boundaries, helping employees manage their time effectively.

- Role Modeling: Encourage leaders to model healthy work-life balance by respecting boundaries and taking time off.

Example Practice

At Tech Solutions Inc., a policy was implemented that discourages emails and work-related messages after 6 PM. This policy, supported by the corporate chaplain, has helped employees disconnect from work and focus on their personal lives.

2. Promoting Personal Well-being Activities

Definition and Importance

Encouraging employees to engage in personal well-being activities helps them recharge and maintain a healthy balance.

Implementation

- Wellness Programs: Develop wellness programs that include physical activities, relaxation techniques, and hobbies.

- Time Management Workshops: Offer workshops on time management and prioritization skills to help employees manage their workloads effectively.

- Personal Development: Provide opportunities for personal development, such as courses and hobbies that employees can pursue outside of work.

Example Practice

Wellness Tech Ltd. offers a comprehensive wellness program that includes fitness classes, relaxation sessions, and personal development courses. This program has significantly improved employees' work-life balance and overall well-being.

Conclusion

Addressing stress, burnout, and work-life balance is essential for maintaining a healthy and productive workforce. Corporate chaplaincy plays a crucial role in providing the support and resources employees need to navigate these challenges. By offering stress management resources, promoting work-life balance, and providing emotional and spiritual support, chaplains can help employees achieve holistic well-being.

As we continue to explore the role of corporate chaplaincy in this book, we will delve into further strategies and best practices for addressing the common issues faced by employees. By understanding and addressing these challenges, organizations can create environments where employees feel valued, supported, and inspired.

Grief, Loss, and Personal Crises

Introduction

Grief, loss, and personal crises are inevitable parts of life that can profoundly affect employees' emotional and mental well-being. These experiences can significantly impact their performance, relationships, and overall presence at work. This chapter explores the common issues faced by employees dealing with grief, loss, and personal crises and offers practical strategies for providing support through corporate chaplaincy.

Understanding Grief and Loss in the Workplace

Definition and Importance

Grief and loss are emotional responses to significant changes or losses, such as the death of a loved one, the end of a relationship, or other major life transitions. These experiences can be deeply personal and affect individuals in various ways.

Types of Loss

1. Death of a Loved One: Losing a family member, friend, or colleague can lead to profound grief and emotional distress.

2. Relationship Changes: Divorce, separation, or the end of a significant relationship can cause emotional turmoil and a sense of loss.

3. Major Life Transitions: Events such as moving, retirement, or significant health changes can trigger feelings of grief and loss.

Effects of Grief and Loss

1. Emotional Impact: Grief can lead to feelings of sadness, anger, guilt, and helplessness.

2. Physical Symptoms: Individuals may experience fatigue, changes in appetite, and sleep disturbances.

3. Cognitive Effects: Grief can impair concentration, decision-making, and memory.

4. Behavioral Changes: Changes in behavior, such as withdrawal, irritability, and decreased motivation, are common.

Addressing Grief and Loss Through Corporate Chaplaincy

1. Providing Emotional Support

Definition and Importance

Providing emotional support helps employees navigate their grief and loss by offering a compassionate and understanding presence.

Implementation

- Active Listening: Offer a listening ear without judgment or unsolicited advice, allowing employees to express their feelings and experiences.

- Empathy and Compassion: Show empathy and compassion, acknowledging the pain and difficulty of their situation.

- Regular Check-Ins: Schedule regular check-ins with grieving employees to offer ongoing support and monitor their well-being.

Example Practice

At Harmony Corp, the corporate chaplain conducts regular one-on-one check-ins with employees experiencing grief and loss. These sessions provide a safe space for employees to express their emotions and receive compassionate support.

2. Offering Grief Counseling and Resources

Definition and Importance

Grief counseling and resources provide employees with professional guidance and tools to cope with their loss and begin the healing process.

Implementation

- Professional Counseling: Provide access to professional grief counselors or therapists who specialize in grief and loss.

- Support Groups: Establish support groups where employees can share their experiences and find comfort in the company of others who understand their pain.

- Educational Resources: Offer books, articles, and online resources that provide information on grief and coping strategies.

Example Practice

Global Enterprises offers access to professional grief counselors through its Employee Assistance Program (EAP). Additionally, the corporate chaplain facilitates monthly support group meetings for employees dealing with loss. These resources have been instrumental in helping employees cope with their grief.

3. Creating a Supportive Work Environment

Definition and Importance

A supportive work environment acknowledges the impact of grief and loss and provides the necessary accommodations and understanding to support grieving employees.

Implementation

- Flexible Work Arrangements: Offer flexible working hours, remote work options, and leave policies to allow employees time to grieve and attend to personal matters.

- Bereavement Leave: Provide paid bereavement leave to give employees the time they need to process their loss and manage related responsibilities.

- Manager Training: Train managers to recognize signs of grief and respond with sensitivity and support.

Example Practice

At Wellness Tech Ltd., managers are trained to support grieving employees, offering flexible work arrangements and paid bereavement leave. This approach has created a compassionate and understanding work environment.

Understanding Personal Crises

Definition and Importance

Personal crises are significant life events that cause intense stress and disruption, such as health issues, financial difficulties, or family emergencies. These crises can have a profound impact on employees' emotional and mental well-being.

Types of Personal Crises

1. Health Issues: Serious illness or injury of the employee or a loved one.

2. Financial Difficulties: Sudden financial hardship, such as job loss of a spouse or unexpected expenses.

3. Family Emergencies: Situations such as a family member's serious illness, legal issues, or other urgent matters.

Effects of Personal Crises

1. Emotional Distress: Intense emotions such as anxiety, fear, and helplessness.

2. Cognitive Impairment: Difficulty concentrating, making decisions, and maintaining focus.

3. Physical Symptoms: Stress-related physical symptoms such as headaches, stomach problems, and fatigue.

4. Behavioral Changes: Changes in behavior, such as withdrawal, irritability, and decreased performance.

Addressing Personal Crises Through Corporate Chaplaincy

1. Providing Immediate Support

Definition and Importance

Offering immediate support during a personal crisis helps employees manage their stress and feel cared for by their organization.

Implementation

- Crisis Intervention: Provide immediate counseling and support to employees facing a personal crisis. This can include one-on-one sessions with a chaplain or counselor.

- Emergency Resources: Offer access to emergency resources, such as financial assistance programs, legal support, and medical care.

- Flexible Policies: Implement flexible policies that allow employees to take time off or adjust their work schedules during a crisis.

Example Practice

At Tech Solutions Inc., the corporate chaplain provides immediate crisis intervention support to employees facing personal emergencies. This includes offering counseling, connecting them with necessary resources, and coordinating with HR to adjust their work schedules as needed.

2. Facilitating Long-Term Support

Definition and Importance

Long-term support ensures that employees continue to receive the help they need as they navigate their personal crises and work towards recovery.

Implementation

- Ongoing Counseling: Offer ongoing counseling and support sessions to help employees cope with the aftermath of a crisis and develop resilience.

- Peer Support Networks: Establish peer support networks where employees can connect with colleagues who have experienced similar challenges.

- Recovery Programs: Develop recovery programs that include resources and workshops on stress management, resilience building, and personal development.

Example Practice

Global Enterprises provides long-term support to employees through ongoing counseling sessions and peer support networks. These initiatives help employees recover from personal crises and rebuild their lives with the support of their workplace community.

3. Promoting a Culture of Compassion and Understanding

Definition and Importance

Promoting a culture of compassion and understanding helps create an environment where employees feel supported and valued, especially during difficult times.

Implementation

- Open Communication: Encourage open communication about personal crises and the available support resources. Ensure employees know they can seek help without stigma or judgment.

- Compassionate Leadership: Train leaders to respond with empathy and support when employees face personal crises. Encourage them to lead by example in fostering a compassionate culture.

- Company Policies: Develop and communicate company policies that prioritize employee well-being and provide clear guidelines for support during personal crises.

Example Practice

At Wellness Tech Ltd., compassionate leadership and open communication are core values. The company regularly communicates about available support resources and encourages leaders to demonstrate empathy and understanding. This approach has created a supportive culture that values employee well-being.

Conclusion

Grief, loss, and personal crises are significant challenges that can deeply affect employees' well-being and performance. Corporate chaplaincy plays a crucial role in providing the support and resources needed to navigate these difficult times. By offering emotional support, counseling, flexible policies, and fostering a culture of compassion, chaplains can help employees cope with grief, loss, and personal crises.

As we continue to explore the role of corporate chaplaincy in this book, we will delve into further strategies and best practices for addressing the common issues faced by employees. By understanding and addressing these challenges, organizations can create environments where employees feel valued, supported, and inspired.

Moral and Ethical Dilemmas

Introduction

In the corporate world, employees often encounter moral and ethical dilemmas that challenge their values, principles, and integrity. These dilemmas can create significant stress and anxiety, impacting their decision-making processes and overall well-being. This chapter explores common moral and ethical dilemmas faced by employees and provides strategies for addressing these challenges through corporate chaplaincy.

Understanding Moral and Ethical Dilemmas

Definition and Importance

Moral and ethical dilemmas arise when individuals face situations where they must choose between conflicting values, principles, or duties. These dilemmas often involve making difficult decisions that have significant consequences for themselves and others.

Types of Moral and Ethical Dilemmas

1. Conflicts of Interest: Situations where personal interests conflict with professional responsibilities.

2. Whistleblowing: The decision to report unethical or illegal activities within the organization.

3. Fair Treatment: Issues related to discrimination, harassment, and equitable treatment of employees.

4. Resource Allocation: Decisions about the fair distribution of resources, opportunities, and rewards.

5. Integrity and Honesty: Situations where employees must choose between honesty and deception, often under pressure to meet goals or expectations.

Effects of Moral and Ethical Dilemmas

1. Emotional Distress: Feelings of guilt, anxiety, and stress resulting from difficult decisions.

2. Cognitive Dissonance: Internal conflict arising from inconsistency between beliefs and actions.

3. Reduced Job Satisfaction: Decreased job satisfaction and engagement due to ethical conflicts.

4. Strained Relationships: Tension and conflict with colleagues, managers, and stakeholders.

Addressing Moral and Ethical Dilemmas Through Corporate Chaplaincy

1. Providing Ethical Guidance and Support

Definition and Importance

Providing ethical guidance and support helps employees navigate moral and ethical dilemmas with confidence and integrity.

Implementation

- Ethical Counseling: Offer one-on-one counseling sessions with a corporate chaplain or ethics advisor to discuss ethical concerns and explore possible solutions.

- Ethics Workshops: Conduct workshops on ethical decision-making, covering topics such as integrity, fairness, and professional responsibility.

- Confidential Helpline: Establish a confidential helpline where employees can seek advice and support on ethical issues.

Example Practice

At Global Enterprises, the corporate chaplain provides ethical counseling sessions for employees facing moral dilemmas. These sessions help employees explore their values, consider the consequences of their decisions, and make choices that align with their principles.

2. Creating a Culture of Integrity

Definition and Importance

Fostering a culture of integrity involves promoting ethical behavior and decision-making throughout the organization.

Implementation

- Ethics Policies: Develop and communicate clear ethics policies that outline expected behaviors and procedures for addressing ethical concerns.

- Leadership Commitment: Encourage leaders to model ethical behavior and demonstrate a commitment to integrity in their actions and decisions.

- Recognition Programs: Recognize and reward employees who demonstrate ethical behavior and make principled decisions.

Example Practice

Wellness Tech Ltd. has established a comprehensive ethics policy and regularly communicates it to employees. Leaders at all levels are trained to model ethical behavior, and employees who demonstrate exceptional integrity are publicly recognized and rewarded.

3. Encouraging Open Dialogue and Reporting

Definition and Importance

Encouraging open dialogue and reporting helps create an environment where employees feel safe to voice their ethical concerns and seek guidance.

Implementation

- Safe Reporting Channels: Provide multiple channels for reporting ethical concerns, such as anonymous hotlines, suggestion boxes, and dedicated email addresses.

- Open Forums: Organize regular open forums where employees can discuss ethical issues and share their experiences in a supportive setting.

- Non-Retaliation Policy: Implement a non-retaliation policy to protect employees who report ethical concerns from retaliation or discrimination.

Example Practice

At Creative Minds Corp, employees are encouraged to report ethical concerns through an anonymous hotline.

Regular open forums are held to discuss ethical issues, and a strict non-retaliation policy is enforced to ensure that employees feel safe and supported.

4. Offering Ethical Decision-Making Frameworks

Definition and Importance

Providing frameworks for ethical decision-making helps employees systematically approach and resolve moral dilemmas.

Implementation

- Decision-Making Models: Introduce decision-making models that guide employees through a structured process for resolving ethical dilemmas. Examples include the Four-Way Test, the PLUS Model, and the Ethical Decision-Making Pyramid.

- Training Programs: Offer training programs that teach employees how to apply these models in real-life situations.

- Case Studies: Use case studies to illustrate the application of ethical decision-making frameworks and facilitate discussions on best practices.

Example Practice

Tech Solutions Inc. has implemented the PLUS Model for ethical decision-making and offers regular training sessions on its application. Employees are encouraged to use this model when faced with moral dilemmas, and case studies are used to reinforce learning.

5. Supporting Whistleblowers

Definition and Importance

Supporting whistleblowers involves providing protection and guidance to employees who report unethical or illegal activities within the organization.

Implementation

- Whistleblower Protection Policy: Develop a whistleblower protection policy that outlines the rights and protections afforded to employees who report concerns.

- Confidential Reporting: Ensure that whistleblowers can report concerns confidentially and anonymously if desired.

- Support Services: Offer support services, such as counseling and legal advice, to whistleblowers to help them navigate the reporting process.

Example Practice

At Harmony Corp, a robust whistleblower protection policy is in place, and employees can report concerns through a confidential hotline. The corporate chaplain provides counseling and support services to whistleblowers, ensuring they feel protected and supported.

Conclusion

Moral and ethical dilemmas are common challenges in the workplace that can significantly impact employees' well-being and performance. Corporate chaplaincy plays a crucial role in providing the guidance, support, and resources needed to navigate these dilemmas with integrity and confidence. By offering ethical counseling, fostering a culture of integrity, encouraging open dialogue, providing decision-making frameworks, and supporting whistleblowers, chaplains can help employees address moral and ethical challenges effectively.

As we continue to explore the role of corporate chaplaincy in this book, we will delve into further strategies and best practices for addressing the common issues faced by employees. By understanding and addressing these challenges, organizations can create environments where employees feel valued, supported, and inspired.

Providing Support

Counseling Techniques for Chaplains

Introduction

Providing effective support to employees through counseling is a fundamental aspect of corporate chaplaincy. Chaplains must be equipped with a variety of counseling techniques to address the diverse needs and challenges employees face. This chapter explores essential counseling techniques that chaplains can use to offer meaningful support, foster trust, and promote well-being among employees.

1. Active Listening

Definition and Importance

Active listening involves fully engaging with the speaker, showing empathy, and understanding their perspective. It is crucial for building trust and ensuring that employees feel heard and valued.

Techniques

- Undivided Attention: Give the speaker your full attention, minimizing distractions and maintaining eye contact.

- Reflective Listening: Reflect back what the speaker has said to confirm understanding and demonstrate empathy. For example, "It sounds like you're feeling overwhelmed by your workload."

- Clarifying Questions: Ask open-ended questions to clarify and deepen your understanding of the speaker's concerns. For example, "Can you tell me more about what's been troubling you?"

- Non-Verbal Cues: Use non-verbal cues, such as nodding and appropriate facial expressions, to show that you are engaged and supportive.

Example Practice

During a counseling session at Harmony Corp, the chaplain listens attentively to an employee discussing their stress about meeting project deadlines. The chaplain reflects back the employee's concerns, asks clarifying questions, and uses supportive non-verbal cues, making the employee feel understood and supported.

2. Empathy and Compassion

Definition and Importance

Empathy involves understanding and sharing the feelings of others, while compassion goes a step further, involving a desire to help alleviate their suffering. These qualities are essential for creating a supportive and healing environment.

Techniques

- Validating Feelings: Acknowledge and validate the employee's feelings. For example, "It's understandable that you're feeling anxious about this situation."

- Expressing Concern: Show genuine concern and a willingness to help. For example, "I'm really sorry that you're going through this. How can I support you?"

- Maintaining a Non-Judgmental Attitude: Approach the employee's concerns without judgment, creating a safe space for them to open up.

Example Practice

At Wellness Tech Ltd., the corporate chaplain meets with an employee who is grieving the loss of a loved one. The chaplain listens empathetically, validates the employee's feelings of sadness, and expresses a desire to support them through their grief.

3. Solution-Focused Counseling

Definition and Importance

Solution-focused counseling emphasizes finding practical solutions to specific problems. It helps employees set goals and develop strategies to overcome challenges.

Techniques

- Goal Setting: Help the employee define clear and achievable goals. For example, "What is one small step you can take this week to reduce your stress?"

- Exploring Strengths: Identify and build on the employee's strengths and resources. For example, "What has helped you manage similar challenges in the past?"

- Developing Action Plans: Work with the employee to create a concrete action plan. For example, "Let's outline the steps you can take to address this issue and set a timeline for each step."

Example Practice

A chaplain at Global Enterprises works with an employee who is struggling with time management. Together, they set specific goals for improving productivity, identify the employee's strengths in organizing tasks, and develop a detailed action plan to implement time management techniques.

4. Cognitive-Behavioral Techniques

Definition and Importance

Cognitive-behavioral techniques (CBT) focus on identifying and changing negative thought patterns and behaviors. These techniques are effective for addressing issues such as anxiety, depression, and stress.

Techniques

- Identifying Negative Thoughts: Help the employee identify negative or unhelpful thoughts. For example, "What thoughts go through your mind when you feel anxious about work?"

- Challenging Negative Thoughts: Encourage the employee to challenge and reframe these thoughts. For example, "What evidence do you have that supports or contradicts this thought?"

- Behavioral Strategies: Develop strategies to change negative behaviors and reinforce positive ones. For example, "Let's identify some healthy coping mechanisms you can use when you start to feel overwhelmed."

Example Practice

At Creative Minds Corp, a chaplain uses cognitive-behavioral techniques to help an employee who experiences anxiety before presentations. They work together to identify the employee's negative thoughts, challenge these thoughts with evidence, and develop strategies for building confidence and reducing anxiety.

5. Narrative Therapy

Definition and Importance

Narrative therapy involves helping employees reframe their experiences and personal narratives in a more positive and empowering way. It emphasizes the importance of the stories we tell about ourselves.

Techniques

- Externalizing Problems: Separate the problem from the person. For example, "Instead of saying you are an anxious person, let's talk about how anxiety affects you."

- Exploring Alternative Stories: Encourage the employee to explore alternative, more empowering narratives. For example, "Can you recall a time when you successfully managed a similar challenge?"

- Reinforcing Positive Narratives: Help the employee build and reinforce positive stories about their strengths and achievements. For example, "It sounds like you showed a lot of resilience in that situation."

Example Practice

A chaplain at Tech Solutions Inc. works with an employee who feels overwhelmed by their workload. Through narrative therapy, the chaplain helps the employee externalize the problem, explore past successes, and develop a more empowering narrative about their ability to manage stress.

6. Spiritual Counseling

Definition and Importance

Spiritual counseling involves addressing the spiritual aspects of an employee's life, and helping them find meaning, purpose, and connection. It can be particularly valuable for those facing existential questions or seeking spiritual growth.

Techniques

- Exploring Beliefs and Values: Discuss the employee's spiritual beliefs and values and how they influence their experiences. For example, "How do your spiritual beliefs help you navigate this challenge?"

- Connecting with Spiritual Practices: Encourage the employee to engage in spiritual practices that bring them peace and clarity. For example, "Would you find it helpful to incorporate meditation or prayer into your daily routine?"

- Providing Spiritual Resources: Offer resources such as books, articles, and connections to spiritual communities that support the employee's spiritual growth.

Example Practice

At Harmony Corp, the corporate chaplain provides spiritual counseling to an employee seeking meaning after a significant life change. They explore the employee's spiritual beliefs, discuss how these beliefs can provide comfort and guidance, and recommend resources for further spiritual growth.

7. Crisis Intervention

Definition and Importance

Crisis intervention involves providing immediate and effective support during a crisis, helping the employee stabilize and cope with the situation.

Techniques

- Immediate Assessment: Quickly assess the severity of the crisis and the employee's immediate needs. For example, "Can you tell me what happened and how you're feeling right now?"

- Emotional Stabilization: Help the employee manage their immediate emotions and reactions. For example, "Let's take a few deep breaths together and focus on calming down."

- Developing a Safety Plan: Create a plan to ensure the employee's safety and well-being. For example, "What steps can we take right now to help you feel safe and supported?"

Example Practice

A chaplain at Wellness Tech Ltd. provides crisis intervention for an employee who has just experienced a traumatic event. They assess the situation, help the employee manage their immediate emotions, and develop a safety plan to ensure the employee's well-being.

Conclusion

Effective counseling techniques are essential for corporate chaplains to provide meaningful support to employees facing a variety of challenges. By employing active listening, empathy, solution-focused counseling, cognitive-behavioral techniques, narrative therapy, spiritual counseling, and crisis intervention, chaplains can help employees navigate their difficulties and promote overall well-being.

As we continue to explore the role of corporate chaplaincy in this book, we will delve into further strategies and best practices for addressing the common issues faced by employees. By understanding and addressing these challenges, organizations can create environments where employees feel valued, supported, and inspired.

Chapter 4: Addressing Employee Needs

Referring Employees to Additional Resources When Necessary

Introduction

Corporate chaplains provide invaluable support to employees, but there are times when the issues faced by employees require specialized help beyond the chaplain's expertise. Knowing when and how to refer employees to additional resources is crucial for ensuring they receive the comprehensive care they need. This chapter explores the importance of referrals, the types of resources available, and practical strategies for making effective referrals.

The Importance of Referrals

1. Comprehensive Support: Referrals ensure that employees receive the specialized support necessary for their unique situations, contributing to their overall well-being.

2. Expertise and Specialization: Certain issues, such as severe mental health conditions, legal problems, or financial crises, require the expertise of trained professionals in those fields.

3. Ethical Responsibility: Chaplains have an ethical responsibility to recognize the limits of their expertise and refer employees to appropriate resources when necessary.

Identifying When to Make a Referral

1. Complex Mental Health Issues

Definition and Importance

Complex mental health issues, such as severe depression, anxiety disorders, bipolar disorder, and substance abuse, require the expertise of mental health professionals.

Signs and Symptoms

- Persistent sadness or hopelessness

- Severe anxiety or panic attacks

- Erratic mood swings

- Signs of substance abuse or addiction

Example

An employee at Harmony Corp confides in the chaplain about experiencing severe depression and suicidal thoughts. Recognizing the severity of the situation, the chaplain refers the employee to a licensed therapist and provides information on emergency mental health services.

2. Legal and Financial Problems

Definition and Importance

Legal and financial problems can create significant stress and require specialized advice and intervention from legal or financial professionals.

Signs and Symptoms

- Legal disputes or concerns

- Financial instability or debt crises

- Issues with housing or employment rights

Example

An employee at Wellness Tech Ltd. is facing eviction due to financial difficulties. The chaplain refers the employee to a financial counselor and a legal aid organization that can provide the necessary support.

3. Health-Related Issues

Definition and Importance

Serious health issues, including chronic illnesses, serious injuries, or the need for specialized medical care, require the expertise of healthcare professionals.

Signs and Symptoms

- Ongoing or severe physical health problems

- Chronic pain or medical conditions

- Concerns about medical treatment or healthcare access

Example

At Global Enterprises, an employee shares concerns about managing a chronic illness. The chaplain refers the employee to a healthcare provider specializing in chronic disease management and provides information about support groups.

Types of Resources for Referrals

1. Mental Health Services

Description

Mental health services include therapists, counselors, psychologists, and psychiatrists who can provide specialized care for mental health conditions.

Resources

- Employee Assistance Programs (EAPs): Many organizations offer EAPs that provide free or low-cost mental health services.

- Local Mental Health Clinics: Community mental health clinics often offer accessible services for various mental health needs.

- Hotlines and Crisis Centers: Suicide prevention hotlines and crisis centers provide immediate support for individuals in distress.

2. Legal Aid Services

Description

Legal aid services offer assistance with legal issues, providing advice, representation, and support for individuals facing legal challenges.

Resources

- Legal Aid Organizations: Non-profit organizations that offer free or low-cost legal services to those in need.

- Pro Bono Lawyers: Lawyers who volunteer their time to assist individuals with legal issues.

- Workplace Legal Services: Some organizations provide access to legal services as part of their employee benefits package.

3. Financial Counseling

Description

Financial counseling services help individuals manage their finances, address debt issues, and create financial stability.

Resources

- Financial Advisors: Professionals who offer advice on managing finances, investments, and debt.

- Credit Counseling Services: Organizations that provide support for managing and reducing debt.

- Workplace Financial Wellness Programs: Programs offered by employers that include financial education and counseling.

4. Healthcare Providers

Description

Healthcare providers include doctors, specialists, and medical facilities that offer treatment and care for physical health conditions.

Resources

- Primary Care Physicians: Doctors who provide general medical care and referrals to specialists.

- Specialists: Medical professionals who specialize in specific areas of healthcare, such as cardiology, oncology, or orthopedics.

- Hospitals and Clinics: Facilities that provide comprehensive medical care and treatment.

5. Support Groups and Community Resources

Description

Support groups and community resources offer peer support, education, and assistance for a wide range of issues, including health, addiction, and personal crises.

Resources

- Support Groups: Groups for individuals dealing with similar issues, such as grief, addiction, or chronic illness.

- Community Organizations: Local non-profits and community centers that provide various support services.

- Online Support Networks: Online forums and groups that offer virtual support and resources.

Making Effective Referrals

1. Building a Resource Network

Definition and Importance

Building a network of reliable and accessible resources ensures that chaplains can make informed and effective referrals.

Implementation

- Research and Vetting: Research and vet potential referral resources to ensure they provide high-quality and reliable services.

- Partnerships: Establish partnerships with local organizations, healthcare providers, and support services to create a robust referral network.

- Resource Directory: Maintain an up-to-date directory of referral resources that includes contact information, services offered, and any eligibility requirements.

Example Practice

At Creative Minds Corp, the corporate chaplain has developed a comprehensive resource directory that includes vetted mental health professionals, legal aid services, and community organizations. This directory is regularly updated and easily accessible.

2. Communicating the Referral

Definition and Importance

Effective communication ensures that the employee understands the referral process and feels supported throughout.

Implementation

- Clear Explanation: Explain the reasons for the referral and how the resource can help. For example, "I believe speaking with a financial counselor can help you manage your current financial challenges."

- Providing Information: Give detailed information about the referral resource, including contact details, what to expect, and how to access the service.

- Follow-Up: Arrange a follow-up meeting to check on the employee's progress and provide additional support if needed.

Example Practice

When referring an employee to a mental health professional, the chaplain at Tech Solutions Inc. provides a clear explanation of the services offered, contact information, and what the employee can expect from the initial session. The chaplain also schedules a follow-up meeting to discuss how the employee is doing.

3. Supporting the Referral Process

Definition and Importance

Supporting the employee through the referral process ensures they feel cared for and reduces any anxiety or uncertainty.

Implementation

- Assistance with Access: Help the employee make initial contact with the referral resource, if needed, by providing assistance with scheduling appointments or navigating access.

- Emotional Support: Offer ongoing emotional support, reassuring the employee that seeking additional help is a positive and courageous step.

- Confidentiality: Maintain confidentiality throughout the referral process, ensuring the employee's privacy is respected.

Example Practice

At Harmony Corp, the chaplain assists an employee in scheduling an appointment with a healthcare provider, offering reassurance and emotional support throughout the process. The chaplain also ensures that all information shared remains confidential.

Conclusion

Referring employees to additional resources when necessary is a critical component of corporate chaplaincy. By recognizing the limits of their expertise and providing referrals to specialized professionals and services, chaplains can ensure that employees receive comprehensive support. Building a robust resource network, effectively communicating referrals, and supporting employees through the process are essential steps in making effective referrals.

As we continue to explore the role of corporate chaplaincy in this book, we will delve into further strategies and best practices for addressing the common issues faced by employees. By understanding and addressing these challenges, organizations can create environments where employees feel valued, supported, and inspired.

Case Management and Follow-Up

Introduction

Effective case management and follow-up are essential components of corporate chaplaincy. These practices ensure that employees receive ongoing support and that their needs are continuously assessed and addressed. This chapter explores the importance of case management and follow-up, offering practical strategies for chaplains to implement these processes effectively.

The Importance of Case Management and Follow-Up

1. Continuous Support: Ensures that employees receive ongoing assistance, helping them navigate challenges over time.

2. Accountability: Keeps track of progress and interventions, ensuring that support measures are effective and adjusted as needed.

3. Holistic Care: Provides a comprehensive approach to employee well-being, addressing multiple aspects of their lives.

4. Building Trust: Demonstrates commitment to the employee's well-being, fostering trust and rapport.

Steps in Effective Case Management

1. Initial Assessment

Definition and Importance

The initial assessment involves understanding the employee's concerns, needs, and goals. This step is crucial for developing an effective support plan.

Implementation

- Detailed Intake: Conduct a thorough intake interview to gather information about the employee's situation, including personal, professional, and any relevant medical or psychological history.

- Establishing Rapport: Build trust and rapport during the initial assessment to encourage open and honest communication.

- Setting Goals: Work with the employee to identify their immediate and long-term goals, ensuring that these are realistic and achievable.

Example Practice

At Harmony Corp, the corporate chaplain conducts comprehensive intake interviews with employees seeking support. This process includes discussing their current challenges, exploring their goals, and establishing a foundation of trust.

2. Developing a Support Plan

Definition and Importance

A support plan outlines the strategies and resources that will be used to address the employee's needs and achieve their goals.

Implementation

- Collaborative Planning: Develop the support plan collaboratively with the employee, ensuring their input and agreement.

- Specific Interventions: Identify specific interventions, such as counseling sessions, referrals to other professionals, or participation in support groups.

- Timelines and Milestones: Establish timelines and milestones to track progress and make adjustments as needed.

Example Practice

The corporate chaplain at Wellness Tech Ltd. works with an employee to develop a personalized support plan. This plan includes regular counseling sessions, participation in a stress management workshop, and a referral to a financial advisor.

3. Implementation and Coordination

Definition and Importance

Implementing and coordinating the support plan involves putting the plan into action and ensuring that all resources and interventions are effectively utilized.

Implementation

- Resource Coordination: Coordinate with various resources and professionals to implement the support plan. This may include scheduling appointments, facilitating introductions, and ensuring that services are accessible.

- Regular Check-Ins: Schedule regular check-ins with the employee to monitor progress and provide additional support as needed.

- Documentation: Keep detailed records of all interactions, interventions, and progress to ensure continuity of care and accountability.

Example Practice

At Global Enterprises, the corporate chaplain coordinates with external counselors, financial advisors, and support groups to implement the employee's support plan. Regular check-ins and detailed documentation ensure that the employee's needs are consistently addressed.

Strategies for Effective Follow-Up

1. Regular Follow-Up Meetings

Definition and Importance

Regular follow-up meetings provide opportunities to review progress, address new concerns, and adjust the support plan as needed.

Implementation

- Scheduled Meetings: Schedule follow-up meetings at regular intervals, such as weekly or bi-weekly, depending on the employee's needs.

- Review and Adjust: Use these meetings to review the employee's progress, celebrate successes, and adjust the support plan as necessary.

- Open Communication: Encourage open communication during follow-up meetings, allowing the employee to express any new concerns or challenges.

Example Practice

The corporate chaplain at Tech Solutions Inc. holds bi-weekly follow-up meetings with employees receiving support. These meetings are used to review progress, make necessary adjustments to the support plan, and ensure that employees feel supported.

2. Tracking Progress

Definition and Importance

Tracking progress involves monitoring the employee's development over time to ensure that the support measures are effective.

Implementation

- Progress Reports: Maintain progress reports that document the employee's achievements, challenges, and any changes in their situation.

- Feedback Mechanisms: Implement feedback mechanisms, such as surveys or informal check-ins, to gather the employee's perspective on the support they are receiving.

- Adjustments: Make adjustments to the support plan based on the tracked progress and feedback received.

Example Practice

At Creative Minds Corp, the corporate chaplain maintains detailed progress reports for each employee receiving support. Feedback is regularly gathered and used to refine and improve the support plan.

3. Providing Continuous Resources and Support

Definition and Importance

Continuous provision of resources and support ensures that employees have ongoing access to the help they need to thrive.

Implementation

- Resource Updates: Regularly update the employee on available resources, such as new support groups, workshops, or community services.

- Ongoing Counseling: Offer ongoing counseling sessions to provide continuous emotional and practical support.

- Encouragement and Motivation: Provide encouragement and motivation to help the employee stay engaged and committed to their progress.

Example Practice

The corporate chaplain at Wellness Tech Ltd. ensures that employees are regularly informed about new resources and opportunities for support. Continuous counseling and motivational support help employees stay focused on their goals.

Addressing Challenges in Case Management and Follow-Up

1. Managing High Caseloads

Definition and Importance

High caseloads can be challenging for chaplains, making it difficult to provide individualized attention to each employee.

Strategies

- Prioritization: Prioritize cases based on urgency and need, ensuring that employees facing the most critical issues receive timely support.

- Delegation: Delegate certain tasks to trained support staff or volunteers to manage the workload effectively.

- Efficiency Tools: Use tools and systems, such as case management software, to streamline processes and improve efficiency.

Example Practice

At Global Enterprises, the corporate chaplain uses case management software to keep track of high caseloads and ensure that each employee receives appropriate attention and support. Delegating administrative tasks to support staff helps manage the workload effectively.

2. Ensuring Confidentiality

Definition and Importance

Maintaining confidentiality is crucial for building trust and ensuring that employees feel safe seeking support.

Strategies

- Secure Documentation: Use secure systems for documenting and storing case information to protect employee privacy.

- Clear Policies: Develop and communicate clear confidentiality policies to employees, outlining how their information will be used and protected.

- Training: Train all staff involved in case management on the importance of confidentiality and the procedures for maintaining it.

Example Practice

At Tech Solutions Inc., the corporate chaplain ensures that all case documentation is stored in a secure, encrypted system. Clear confidentiality policies are communicated to employees, and staff are trained to handle sensitive information appropriately.

3. Addressing Resistance to Follow-Up

Definition and Importance

Some employees may be resistant to follow-up, either due to fear, stigma, or a belief that they no longer need support.

Strategies

- Building Trust: Continue to build trust and rapport with the employee, emphasizing the benefits of follow-up support.

- Flexibility: Offer flexible follow-up options, such as virtual meetings or informal check-ins, to accommodate the employee's preferences.

- Encouragement: Provide gentle encouragement and reassurance, helping the employee see the value of ongoing support.

Example Practice

The corporate chaplain at Harmony Corp encounters resistance from an employee who feels they no longer need support. The chaplain offers flexible follow-up options and provides gentle encouragement, eventually helping the employee see the benefits of continued support.

Conclusion

Effective case management and follow-up are critical components of corporate chaplaincy. By conducting thorough initial assessments, developing personalized support plans, coordinating resources, and maintaining regular follow-ups, chaplains can ensure that employees receive comprehensive and continuous support. Addressing challenges such as high caseloads, maintaining confidentiality, and overcoming resistance to follow-up is essential for providing effective care.

As we continue to explore the role of corporate chaplaincy in this book, we will delve into further strategies and best practices for addressing the common issues faced by employees. By understanding and addressing these challenges, organizations can create environments where employees feel valued, supported, and inspired.

CHAPTER 05

CHAPLAINCY AND DIVERSITY

Understanding and Respecting Diversity

Introduction

In today's globalized and interconnected world, workplaces are increasingly diverse, comprising individuals from various cultural, religious, and ethnic backgrounds. For corporate chaplains, understanding and respecting this diversity is paramount. This chapter explores the importance of cultural and religious sensitivity, providing strategies for chaplains to effectively navigate and support a diverse workforce.

The Importance of Cultural and Religious Sensitivity

1. Building Trust and Rapport

Definition and Importance

Cultural and religious sensitivity involves recognizing, respecting, and valuing the diverse backgrounds and beliefs of individuals. This sensitivity is essential for building trust and rapport, which are foundational to effective chaplaincy.

Impact

- Enhanced Communication: Understanding cultural nuances and religious beliefs improves communication and helps avoid misunderstandings.

- Increased Trust: Employees are more likely to seek support from chaplains who respect and understand their cultural and religious contexts.

- Stronger Relationships: Sensitivity to diversity fosters stronger, more authentic relationships between chaplains and employees.

Example

At Global Enterprises, the corporate chaplain makes an effort to learn about the cultural and religious backgrounds of the employees. This knowledge allows the chaplain to connect more deeply with employees, building trust and rapport.

2. Promoting Inclusivity and Respect

Definition and Importance

Promoting inclusivity and respect means creating an environment where all employees feel valued and accepted, regardless of their cultural or religious background.

Impact

- Positive Work Environment: Inclusivity and respect contribute to a positive, supportive work environment where employees feel safe and valued.

- Employee Engagement: When employees feel respected and included, they are more engaged and committed to their work.

- Diverse Perspectives: Valuing diversity brings a range of perspectives and ideas, fostering innovation and creativity.

Example

At Wellness Tech Ltd., the corporate chaplain organizes events celebrating various cultural and religious holidays. These events promote inclusivity and respect, fostering a positive and cohesive work environment.

3. Addressing Discrimination and Bias

Definition and Importance

Addressing discrimination and bias involves recognizing and challenging prejudiced attitudes and behaviors in the workplace. Chaplains play a crucial role in advocating for fair treatment and equality.

Impact

- Fair Treatment: Ensures that all employees are treated equitably and with respect.

- Conflict Resolution: Helps resolve conflicts arising from cultural or religious misunderstandings, promoting harmony.

- Ethical Workplace: Fosters an ethical workplace culture where discrimination and bias are not tolerated.

Example

The corporate chaplain at Tech Solutions Inc. works with HR to develop training programs on unconscious bias and cultural competency. These programs help employees recognize and address their biases, promoting a more inclusive and respectful workplace.

Strategies for Cultural and Religious Sensitivity

1. Education and Training

Definition and Importance

Education and training on cultural and religious sensitivity equip chaplains with the knowledge and skills needed to support a diverse workforce.

Implementation

- Cultural Competency Training: Participate in cultural competency training programs to understand different cultural norms, values, and communication styles.

- Religious Literacy: Learn about various religious beliefs, practices, and holidays to provide appropriate support and accommodations.

- Ongoing Learning: Stay informed about current issues related to diversity, equity, and inclusion through continuous education and professional development.

Example Practice

At Creative Minds Corp, the corporate chaplain attends regular cultural competency workshops and religious literacy seminars. This ongoing education enhances the chaplain's ability to support the diverse needs of employees.

2. Active Listening and Empathy

Definition and Importance

Active listening and empathy involve fully engaging with employees, understanding their perspectives, and showing compassion and respect for their experiences.

Implementation

- Listening Skills: Practice active listening by giving full attention to the speaker, avoiding interruptions, and reflecting back what is heard.

- Empathetic Responses: Show empathy by acknowledging the employee's feelings and experiences without judgment. For example, "I understand that observing your religious practices is very important to you."

- Non-Verbal Cues: Use non-verbal cues, such as nodding and appropriate facial expressions, to demonstrate understanding and support.

Example Practice

The corporate chaplain at Harmony Corp uses active listening and empathetic responses during counseling sessions with employees from diverse backgrounds. This approach helps employees feel heard and respected.

3. Creating Inclusive Policies and Practices

Definition and Importance

Creating inclusive policies and practices ensures that the workplace accommodates the diverse needs of all employees, promoting equality and respect.

Implementation

- Flexible Scheduling: Implement flexible scheduling policies to accommodate religious observances and cultural practices.

- Inclusive Holiday Policies: Recognize and celebrate a variety of cultural and religious holidays, allowing employees to take time off for significant observances.

- Diversity Committees: Establish diversity committees or task forces to advocate for inclusive policies and practices within the organization.

Example Practice

At Global Enterprises, the corporate chaplain collaborates with HR to develop flexible scheduling policies that allow employees to observe religious holidays. This inclusive approach respects employees' cultural and religious practices.

4. Providing Diverse Resources and Support

Definition and Importance

Providing resources and support tailored to the diverse needs of employees helps create a supportive and inclusive work environment.

Implementation

- Resource Materials: Offer books, articles, and online resources on various cultural and religious topics in the company library or resource center.

- Support Groups: Facilitate support groups for employees from specific cultural or religious backgrounds, providing a safe space for sharing and support.

- Referral Networks: Develop a referral network of external resources, such as cultural organizations and religious leaders, to provide additional support.

Example Practice

At Wellness Tech Ltd., the corporate chaplain ensures that the company library includes a wide range of resources on different cultures and religions. Additionally, support groups are available for employees to connect and share their experiences.

5. Engaging with the Community

Definition and Importance

Engaging with the community involves building relationships with local cultural and religious organizations, and enhancing the support network available to employees.

Implementation

- Community Partnerships: Establish partnerships with local cultural and religious organizations to provide resources, support, and educational opportunities.

- Community Events: Participate in or host community events that celebrate cultural and religious diversity, fostering connections between the workplace and the broader community.

- Guest Speakers: Invite guest speakers from various cultural and religious backgrounds to share their insights and experiences with employees.

Example Practice

The corporate chaplain at Creative Minds Corp partners with local cultural organizations to host events celebrating cultural diversity. These events strengthen the connection between the company and the community, promoting mutual understanding and respect.

Conclusion

Understanding and respecting diversity is essential for corporate chaplains to effectively support a diverse workforce. By promoting cultural and religious sensitivity, chaplains can build trust, foster inclusivity, and address discrimination and bias. Through education and training, active listening and empathy, inclusive policies and practices, diverse resources and support, and community engagement, chaplains can create a supportive and inclusive work environment where all employees feel valued and respected.

As we continue to explore the role of corporate chaplaincy in this book, we will delve into further strategies and best practices for addressing the common issues faced by employees. By understanding and addressing these challenges, organizations can create environments where employees feel valued, supported, and inspired.

Building an Inclusive Spiritual Program

Introduction

Creating an inclusive spiritual program in the workplace involves developing initiatives that respect and celebrate the diverse spiritual beliefs and practices of employees. Such programs can enhance well-being, foster a sense of belonging, and promote a positive work environment. This chapter outlines the essential steps and strategies for building an inclusive spiritual program that meets the needs of a diverse workforce.

The Importance of an Inclusive Spiritual Program

1. Fostering Belonging and Inclusivity

Definition and Importance

An inclusive spiritual program recognizes and honors the diverse spiritual beliefs and practices of all employees. It fosters a sense of belonging and ensures that everyone feels respected and included.

Impact

- Enhanced Morale: Employees feel valued and respected, leading to higher morale and job satisfaction.

- Positive Culture: Promotes a workplace culture of inclusivity, respect, and understanding.

- Reduced Conflict: Minimizes misunderstandings and conflicts related to spiritual and religious differences.

Example

At Global Enterprises, the inclusive spiritual program includes celebrations of various religious holidays and the provision of spaces for different spiritual practices. This approach fosters a positive and inclusive workplace culture.

2. Supporting Employee Well-Being

Definition and Importance

Supporting spiritual well-being is essential for holistic employee care. An inclusive spiritual program addresses the spiritual needs of employees, contributing to their overall well-being.

Impact

- Improved Mental Health: Provides employees with resources and support to enhance their mental and emotional well-being.

- Increased Engagement: Employees who feel supported in their spiritual lives are more engaged and productive.

- Stronger Community: Builds a sense of community and mutual support among employees.

Example

Wellness Tech Ltd. has implemented a spiritual well-being program that includes meditation sessions, spiritual counseling, and access to religious resources. This program has significantly improved employee well-being and engagement.

Steps to Building an Inclusive Spiritual Program

1. Conducting a Needs Assessment

Definition and Importance

A needs assessment helps identify the diverse spiritual needs and preferences of employees, ensuring that the program is relevant and effective.

Implementation

- Surveys and Questionnaires: Distribute surveys and questionnaires to gather information on employees' spiritual beliefs, practices, and needs.

- Focus Groups: Organize focus groups to discuss spiritual needs and gather detailed insights.

- Individual Interviews: Conduct one-on-one interviews with employees to understand their personal spiritual needs and preferences.

Example Practice

At Creative Minds Corp, the corporate chaplain conducts an annual survey to assess the spiritual needs of employees. The survey results guide the development of new initiatives and the improvement of existing programs.

2. Developing Inclusive Policies and Practices

Definition and Importance

Inclusive policies and practices ensure that the spiritual program respects and accommodates the diverse spiritual beliefs and practices of employees.

Implementation

- Flexible Scheduling: Implement flexible scheduling policies to accommodate religious observances and spiritual practices.

- Inclusive Holiday Policies: Recognize and celebrate a variety of religious and cultural holidays, allowing employees to take time off for significant observances.

- Accommodations for Practices: Provide accommodations for spiritual practices, such as prayer rooms, meditation spaces, and dietary considerations.

Example Practice

Global Enterprises has developed policies that allow employees to take time off for religious holidays and provide spaces for prayer and meditation. These accommodations support the diverse spiritual needs of employees.

3. Creating Diverse Spiritual Resources

Definition and Importance

Providing diverse spiritual resources ensures that employees have access to materials and support that align with their spiritual beliefs and practices.

Implementation

- Resource Libraries: Establish a library with books, articles, and online resources on various spiritual and religious topics.

- Digital Resources: Offer digital resources, such as e-books, podcasts, and meditation apps, that employees can access at their convenience.

- Guest Speakers and Workshops: Invite guest speakers from different spiritual backgrounds and organize workshops on various spiritual topics.

Example Practice

Wellness Tech Ltd. maintains a comprehensive spiritual resource library that includes materials on different religions and spiritual practices. The company also hosts monthly workshops led by guest speakers from diverse spiritual traditions.

4. Facilitating Inclusive Events and Activities

Definition and Importance

Inclusive events and activities provide opportunities for employees to explore and celebrate their spirituality in a supportive and respectful environment.

Implementation

- Interfaith Celebrations: Organize events that celebrate multiple religious and spiritual holidays, fostering inclusivity and mutual respect.

- Mindfulness and Meditation Sessions: Offer regular mindfulness and meditation sessions that are inclusive of various spiritual practices.

- Community Service Projects: Encourage participation in community service projects that align with diverse spiritual values and promote a sense of purpose and connection.

Example Practice

Creative Minds Corp organizes interfaith celebrations that recognize major religious holidays such as Diwali, Christmas, Ramadan, and Passover. These events foster inclusivity and allow employees to share their traditions and practices.

5. Providing Spiritual Counseling and Support

Definition and Importance

Spiritual counseling and support services help employees navigate personal and professional challenges from a spiritual perspective.

Implementation

- One-on-One Counseling: Offer confidential spiritual counseling sessions with a corporate chaplain or trained spiritual advisor.

- Support Groups: Facilitate support groups for employees to share their spiritual journeys and find mutual support.

- Employee Assistance Programs (EAPs): Integrate spiritual counseling into the company's EAP, offering holistic support for employees.

Example Practice

At Global Enterprises, the corporate chaplain provides one-on-one spiritual counseling and facilitates support groups for employees. These services offer valuable support and guidance, helping employees navigate challenges and enhance their spiritual well-being.

6. Encouraging Employee Involvement

Definition and Importance

Involving employees in the development and implementation of the spiritual program ensures that it meets their needs and fosters a sense of ownership and engagement.

Implementation

- Feedback Mechanisms: Use surveys, suggestion boxes, and focus groups to gather employee feedback on the spiritual program.

- Employee Committees: Establish committees or task forces that include employee representatives to help plan and implement spiritual initiatives.

- Volunteer Opportunities: Encourage employees to volunteer to lead or participate in spiritual activities and events.

Example Practice

Wellness Tech Ltd. has established an employee committee that helps plan and implement the company's spiritual program. This committee includes representatives from various departments and spiritual backgrounds, ensuring diverse perspectives and involvement.

Conclusion

Building an inclusive spiritual program is essential for fostering a positive and supportive work environment. By conducting a needs assessment, developing inclusive policies, creating diverse resources, facilitating inclusive events, providing spiritual counseling, and encouraging employee involvement, organizations can ensure that their spiritual programs respect and celebrate the diverse beliefs and practices of all employees.

As we continue to explore the role of corporate chaplaincy in this book, we will delve into further strategies and best practices for addressing the common issues faced by employees. By understanding and addressing these challenges, organizations can create environments where employees feel valued, supported, and inspired.

Addressing the Needs of a Diverse Workforce

Introduction

In today's globalized workplace, diversity is not only a reality but also an asset that brings a wealth of perspectives, ideas, and experiences. Addressing the needs of a diverse workforce requires a commitment to understanding, respecting, and celebrating this diversity. This chapter outlines strategies for corporate chaplains to effectively support a diverse workforce, ensuring that all employees feel valued and included.

The Importance of Addressing Diversity

1. Enhancing Employee Well-Being

Definition and Importance

Recognizing and addressing the diverse needs of employees enhances their overall well-being, leading to higher job satisfaction and productivity.

Impact

- Inclusive Support: Tailoring support to meet diverse needs ensures that all employees receive the care they need.

- Higher Engagement: Employees who feel understood and valued are more likely to be engaged and committed to their work.

- Improved Mental Health: Providing culturally sensitive support can significantly improve mental health outcomes for employees.

Example

At Global Enterprises, the corporate chaplain offers personalized support that considers employees' cultural and religious backgrounds, leading to higher job satisfaction and well-being.

2. Fostering an Inclusive Work Environment

Definition and Importance

An inclusive work environment values and respects the diversity of all employees, promoting a culture of acceptance and belonging.

Impact

- Positive Culture: An inclusive environment fosters a positive workplace culture where employees feel respected and valued.

- Reduced Turnover: Inclusivity reduces turnover rates by creating a supportive and welcoming workplace.

- Enhanced Collaboration: A diverse and inclusive environment encourages collaboration and innovation by leveraging a variety of perspectives.

Example

Wellness Tech Ltd. promotes an inclusive culture by celebrating diverse holidays, offering flexible work arrangements, and ensuring that all voices are heard and respected.

Strategies for Supporting a Diverse Workforce

1. Cultural Competency Training

Definition and Importance

Cultural competency training equips chaplains and employees with the skills and knowledge to understand, respect, and work effectively with diverse populations.

Implementation

- Regular Training: Offer regular cultural competency training sessions for chaplains and employees to enhance their understanding of diverse cultures and practices.

- Interactive Workshops: Conduct interactive workshops that include role-playing, case studies, and group discussions to deepen cultural awareness.

- Continuous Learning: Encourage ongoing learning and development in cultural competency through seminars, webinars, and online courses.

Example Practice

At Creative Minds Corp, the corporate chaplain organizes quarterly cultural competency workshops that include interactive activities and discussions. These workshops help employees and chaplains develop a deeper understanding of cultural diversity.

2. Celebrating Cultural and Religious Diversity

Definition and Importance

Celebrating cultural and religious diversity acknowledges and honors the different backgrounds and beliefs of employees, fostering a sense of belonging.

Implementation

- Holiday Celebrations: Organize events and activities to celebrate a variety of cultural and religious holidays, ensuring inclusivity and participation.

- Educational Programs: Offer educational programs and materials that highlight the significance of different cultural and religious traditions.

- Inclusive Communication: Use inclusive language in all communications and recognize diverse holidays in company calendars and announcements.

Example Practice

Global Enterprises celebrates major religious and cultural holidays such as Diwali, Ramadan, Hanukkah, and Lunar New Year. These celebrations include educational sessions, festive activities, and opportunities for employees to share their traditions.

3. Providing Culturally Sensitive Support

Definition and Importance

Culturally sensitive support involves understanding and respecting the cultural contexts of employees' experiences and providing appropriate care and resources.

Implementation

- Tailored Counseling: Offer counseling services that are sensitive to the cultural and religious backgrounds of employees, ensuring that their unique needs are met.

- Language Services: Provide translation and interpretation services to support employees who are not fluent in the primary language of the workplace.

- Community Resources: Connect employees with community resources and organizations that offer culturally relevant support and services.

Example Practice

The corporate chaplain at Wellness Tech Ltd. offers counseling sessions in multiple languages and collaborates with community organizations to provide culturally relevant resources for employees.

4. Developing Inclusive Policies and Practices

Definition and Importance

Inclusive policies and practices ensure that the workplace accommodates and respects the diverse needs of all employees.

Implementation

- Flexible Work Arrangements: Implement policies that allow for flexible work hours and remote work to accommodate diverse needs, such as religious observances and family responsibilities.

- Non-Discrimination Policies: Develop and enforce policies that prohibit discrimination based on race, religion, gender, sexual orientation, and other characteristics.

- Diversity and Inclusion Committees: Establish committees to advocate for and oversee the implementation of diversity and inclusion initiatives.

Example Practice

At Creative Minds Corp, the corporate chaplain works with HR to develop flexible scheduling policies that accommodate religious observances and family responsibilities. The company also has a diversity and inclusion committee that promotes inclusive practices and policies.

5. Encouraging Open Dialogue and Feedback

Definition and Importance

Encouraging open dialogue and feedback helps identify and address the diverse needs of employees, fostering an inclusive and responsive workplace culture.

Implementation

- Feedback Mechanisms: Use surveys, suggestion boxes, and focus groups to gather feedback on diversity and inclusion efforts.

- Open Forums: Organize open forums and town hall meetings where employees can discuss their experiences and offer suggestions for improvement.

- Responsive Action: Act on the feedback received to continuously improve diversity and inclusion initiatives and address any concerns raised by employees.

Example Practice

At Global Enterprises, the corporate chaplain holds quarterly town hall meetings to discuss diversity and inclusion. Feedback from these meetings is used to refine and enhance the company's diversity initiatives.

Conclusion

Addressing the needs of a diverse workforce is essential for creating an inclusive and supportive workplace. By providing cultural competency training, celebrating cultural and religious diversity, offering culturally sensitive support, developing inclusive policies and practices, and encouraging open dialogue and feedback, corporate chaplains can effectively support a diverse workforce. These strategies not only enhance employee well-being but also foster a positive and inclusive work environment.

As we continue to explore the role of corporate chaplaincy in this book, we will delve into further strategies and best practices for addressing the common issues faced by

employees. By understanding and addressing these challenges, organizations can create environments where employees feel valued, supported, and inspired.

Interfaith Chaplaincy

Principles of Interfaith Work

Introduction

Interfaith chaplaincy involves providing spiritual support to individuals from diverse religious backgrounds. This approach requires a deep understanding and respect for different faith traditions and the ability to offer inclusive and non-sectarian support. This chapter explores the principles of interfaith work and provides strategies for chaplains to effectively navigate and support a religiously diverse workforce.

The Importance of Interfaith Chaplaincy

1. Respect for Diversity

Definition and Importance

Interfaith chaplaincy respects and values the diversity of religious beliefs and practices among employees. It fosters an environment where all faith traditions are honored and included.

Impact

- Inclusive Support: Ensures that spiritual support is accessible to all employees, regardless of their religious background.

- Mutual Respect: Promotes mutual respect and understanding among employees of different faiths.

- Enhanced Well-Being: Supports the spiritual well-being of a diverse workforce by acknowledging and respecting their unique religious needs.

Example

At Global Enterprises, the corporate chaplain offers interfaith support, ensuring that employees from various religious backgrounds receive the care and respect they deserve.

2. Building Bridges Between Faiths

Definition and Importance

Interfaith chaplaincy builds bridges between different faith traditions, promoting dialogue, understanding, and collaboration.

Impact

- Community Building: Fosters a sense of community and unity among employees of different faiths.

- Conflict Resolution: Helps resolve conflicts that may arise from religious misunderstandings or differences.

- Cultural Competence: Enhances cultural competence by encouraging employees to learn about and appreciate different faith traditions.

Example

Wellness Tech Ltd. hosts interfaith dialogue sessions facilitated by the corporate chaplain. These sessions provide opportunities for employees to share their beliefs and learn from one another, building a cohesive and understanding community.

Principles of Interfaith Work

1. Respect and Inclusivity

Definition and Importance

Respect and inclusivity are foundational principles of interfaith work. They involve honoring the beliefs and practices of all faith traditions and ensuring that everyone feels included and valued.

Implementation

- Non-Judgmental Approach: Approach all faith traditions with respect and without judgment. Recognize the value and dignity of each belief system.

- Inclusive Language: Use inclusive language that respects all religious beliefs and avoids privileging one faith over another.

- Cultural Sensitivity: Be aware of and sensitive to the cultural contexts of different faith traditions, including their rituals, symbols, and practices.

Example Practice

At Creative Minds Corp, the corporate chaplain uses inclusive language in all communications and ensures that spiritual support services respect and honor the diverse religious beliefs of employees.

2. Education and Awareness

Definition and Importance

Education and awareness involve learning about different faith traditions to provide informed and respectful support.

Implementation

- Ongoing Education: Engage in continuous learning about various religious beliefs, practices, and holidays. Attend workshops, read relevant literature, and participate in interfaith training programs.

- Educational Resources: Provide employees with educational resources about different faith traditions to promote understanding and respect.

- Interfaith Events: Organize events that educate employees about different religions, such as interfaith panels, guest speakers, and cultural celebrations.

Example Practice

Global Enterprises offers a range of educational resources on different religions and regularly hosts interfaith events that educate employees and promote mutual understanding.

3. Dialogue and Communication

Definition and Importance

Dialogue and communication are essential for fostering understanding and collaboration between different faith traditions.

Implementation

- Interfaith Dialogue Sessions: Facilitate regular interfaith dialogue sessions where employees can share their beliefs and experiences in a respectful and open environment.

- Active Listening: Practice active listening during interfaith interactions, showing empathy and understanding for different perspectives.

- Conflict Resolution: Use dialogue as a tool for resolving conflicts that may arise from religious differences, promoting harmony and mutual respect.

Example Practice

At Wellness Tech Ltd., the corporate chaplain facilitates monthly interfaith dialogue sessions, providing a platform for employees to discuss their beliefs and learn from one another.

4. Collaboration and Partnership

Definition and Importance

Collaboration and partnership involve working together with representatives from different faith traditions to create a supportive and inclusive environment.

Implementation

- Interfaith Committees: Establish interfaith committees that include representatives from various religious backgrounds to guide the development of inclusive policies and practices.

- Community Partnerships: Partner with local religious and interfaith organizations to provide additional resources and support for employees.

- Shared Initiatives: Collaborate on initiatives that promote interfaith understanding and cooperation, such as community service projects and interfaith workshops.

Example Practice

Creative Minds Corp has an interfaith committee that includes employees from different religious backgrounds. This committee helps develop policies and initiatives that promote inclusivity and respect for all faith traditions.

5. Spiritual Care and Support

Definition and Importance

Providing spiritual care and support involves offering resources and services that meet the diverse spiritual needs of employees.

Implementation

- Inclusive Spiritual Counseling: Offer spiritual counseling that respects and incorporates the diverse religious beliefs of employees.

- Resource Provision: Provide access to religious texts, prayer spaces, and other resources that support various faith practices.

- Support Groups: Facilitate interfaith support groups where employees can share their spiritual journeys and find mutual support.

Example Practice

At Global Enterprises, the corporate chaplain provides inclusive spiritual counseling and facilitates interfaith support groups, ensuring that all employees have access to the spiritual care they need.

Challenges and Solutions in Interfaith Work

1. Navigating Religious Differences

Definition and Importance

Navigating religious differences can be challenging but is essential for fostering a respectful and inclusive environment.

Challenges

- Misunderstandings: Misunderstandings and misconceptions about different religions can lead to conflict and division.

- Stereotypes and Bias: Stereotypes and biases about certain religions can create barriers to understanding and respect.

Solutions

- Education and Awareness: Promote education and awareness to dispel myths and misconceptions about different religions.

- Open Dialogue: Encourage open and respectful dialogue to address misunderstandings and build mutual respect.

- Bias Training: Provide training on unconscious bias to help employees recognize and overcome their biases.

Example Practice

At Creative Minds Corp, the corporate chaplain provides bias training and facilitates open dialogue sessions to address religious misunderstandings and promote mutual respect.

2. Balancing Diverse Needs

Definition and Importance

Balancing the diverse needs of employees from different religious backgrounds requires careful planning and sensitivity.

Challenges

- Conflicting Practices: Different religious practices and observances may conflict, creating challenges in scheduling and accommodations.

- Resource Allocation: Ensuring that resources and support are equitably distributed among employees from different faith backgrounds.

Solutions

- Flexible Policies: Implement flexible policies that accommodate diverse religious practices and observances.

- Equitable Resource Distribution: Ensure that resources and support are distributed equitably, respecting the needs of all employees.

Example Practice

Global Enterprises implements flexible scheduling policies to accommodate religious observances and ensures that prayer spaces and other resources are available to employees from all faith backgrounds.

Conclusion

Interfaith chaplaincy is essential for providing inclusive and respectful spiritual support to a diverse workforce. By adhering to principles of respect and inclusivity, education and awareness, dialogue and communication, collaboration and partnership, and providing spiritual care and support, chaplains can effectively navigate the complexities of interfaith work. Addressing challenges such as navigating religious differences and balancing diverse needs is crucial for fostering a supportive and inclusive work environment.

As we continue to explore the role of corporate chaplaincy in this book, we will delve into further strategies and best practices for addressing the common issues faced by employees. By understanding and addressing these challenges, organizations can create environments where employees feel valued, supported, and inspired.

Creating Spaces for Multiple Faith Traditions

Introduction

Providing spaces that accommodate multiple faith traditions is crucial for fostering an inclusive and respectful workplace. These spaces allow employees to practice their religious and spiritual beliefs comfortably and with dignity. This chapter explores strategies for creating and maintaining spaces that support the diverse spiritual needs of employees, ensuring that everyone feels valued and respected.

The Importance of Multi-Faith Spaces

1. Promoting Inclusivity and Respect

Definition and Importance

Creating multi-faith spaces involves designing areas that are welcoming and accessible to individuals from all religious backgrounds. These spaces promote inclusivity and respect for diversity within the workplace.

Impact

- Inclusive Environment: Demonstrates a commitment to inclusivity and respect for all faith traditions.

- Employee Well-Being: Supports the spiritual well-being of employees by providing a designated area for religious and spiritual practices.

- Enhanced Morale: Fosters a sense of belonging and respect, leading to higher employee morale and engagement.

Example

At Global Enterprises, the creation of a multi-faith prayer room has significantly enhanced the inclusivity of the workplace, allowing employees from various religious backgrounds to practice their faith in a respectful environment.

2. Supporting Diverse Spiritual Practices

Definition and Importance

Multi-faith spaces accommodate a variety of spiritual practices, ensuring that all employees can observe their religious rituals and traditions.

Impact

- Accessibility: Provides a convenient and accessible space for employees to engage in their spiritual practices.

- Flexibility: Offers flexibility to accommodate different religious observances and practices.

- Community Building: Encourages a sense of community among employees who share similar spiritual needs.

Example

Wellness Tech Ltd. has designated a multi-faith space that includes separate areas for prayer, meditation, and reflection, supporting a range of spiritual practices and fostering a sense of community among employees.

Strategies for Creating Multi-Faith Spaces

1. Consulting with Employees

Definition and Importance

Consulting with employees ensures that the design and implementation of multi-faith spaces meet the diverse needs and preferences of the workforce.

Implementation

- Surveys and Focus Groups: Conduct surveys and focus groups to gather input from employees about their needs and preferences for a multi-faith space.

- Feedback Mechanisms: Establish ongoing feedback mechanisms, such as suggestion boxes and regular check-ins, to continuously improve the space.

- Inclusive Planning: Involve representatives from different faith traditions in the planning and design process.

Example Practice

At Creative Minds Corp, the corporate chaplain conducts focus groups with employees from various religious backgrounds to gather input on the design and features of the multi-faith space. This collaborative approach ensures that the space meets diverse needs.

2. Designing Flexible and Adaptable Spaces

Definition and Importance

Designing flexible and adaptable multi-faith spaces ensures that the area can accommodate a variety of spiritual practices and needs.

Implementation

- Modular Design: Use modular furniture and movable partitions to create a flexible space that can be easily reconfigured for different uses.

- Neutral Decor: Choose neutral colors and decor to create a welcoming and inclusive environment for all faith traditions.

- Accessibility: Ensure that the space is easily accessible to all employees, including those with disabilities.

Example Practice

Global Enterprises uses modular furniture and movable partitions in their multi-faith space, allowing the area to be easily adapted for different religious practices and events. The neutral decor and accessible design create a welcoming environment for all employees.

3. Providing Essential Resources

Definition and Importance

Providing essential resources ensures that employees have the tools and materials they need to engage in their spiritual practices comfortably.

Implementation

- Prayer Mats and Cushions: Provide prayer mats, cushions, and other items needed for different religious practices.

- Religious Texts: Offer a selection of religious texts and literature in the multi-faith space.

- Cleaning Facilities: Include facilities for ablution and washing, such as sinks and foot baths, for religions that require ritual cleansing before prayer.

Example Practice

Wellness Tech Ltd. equips its multi-faith space with prayer mats, cushions, and a variety of religious texts. The space also includes a small washing area for ritual cleansing, ensuring that employees have the resources they need for their spiritual practices.

4. Establishing Guidelines for Use

Definition and Importance

Establishing clear guidelines for the use of multi-faith spaces ensures that the area is respected and maintained appropriately.

Implementation

- Usage Policies: Develop policies that outline the appropriate use of the space, including scheduling, cleanliness, and respectful behavior.

- Signage and Information: Provide clear signage and information about the guidelines and available resources in the multi-faith space.

- Monitoring and Maintenance: Assign responsibility for monitoring and maintaining the space to ensure it remains clean, respectful, and accessible.

Example Practice

At Creative Minds Corp, the corporate chaplain develops usage policies for the multi-faith space, including guidelines for scheduling, cleanliness, and respectful behavior. Clear signage and regular maintenance ensure that the space is respected and well-maintained.

5. Encouraging Participation and Engagement

Definition and Importance

Encouraging participation and engagement helps ensure that the multi-faith space is actively used and valued by employees.

Implementation

- Awareness Campaigns: Promote the availability and benefits of the multi-faith space through awareness campaigns, newsletters, and informational sessions.

- Events and Activities: Organize events and activities that encourage employees to use the space, such as interfaith dialogues, meditation sessions, and cultural celebrations.

- Feedback and Improvement: Continuously gather feedback from employees and make improvements to the space based on their suggestions and needs.

Example Practice

Global Enterprises promotes the multi-faith space through regular awareness campaigns and organizes events such as interfaith dialogues and meditation sessions. Continuous feedback is gathered to ensure the space meets the evolving needs of employees.

Challenges and Solutions in Creating Multi-Faith Spaces

1. Balancing Diverse Needs

Definition and Importance

Balancing the diverse needs of different faith traditions can be challenging but is essential for creating an inclusive space.

Challenges

- Conflicting Practices: Different religious practices and observances may conflict, creating challenges in scheduling and usage.

- Resource Allocation: Ensuring that resources and support are equitably distributed among different faith traditions.

Solutions

- Flexible Scheduling: Implement flexible scheduling policies that allow for shared use of the space and accommodate different religious observances.

- Equitable Resource Distribution: Ensure that resources and support are equitably distributed, respecting the needs of all faith traditions.

Example Practice

At Creative Minds Corp, the corporate chaplain implements a scheduling system that allows for shared use of the multi-faith space, ensuring that all religious practices can be accommodated. Resources are equitably distributed to respect the needs of all employees.

2. Maintaining Neutrality and Respect

Definition and Importance

Maintaining neutrality and respect in the multi-faith space ensures that it remains welcoming and inclusive for all employees.

Challenges

- Religious Symbols: Displaying religious symbols and artifacts that may not be inclusive of all faith traditions.

- Respectful Behavior: Ensuring that all employees use the space respectfully and adhere to established guidelines.

Solutions

- Neutral Decor: Use neutral decor and avoid displaying specific religious symbols that may not be inclusive.

- Guidelines and Education: Establish clear guidelines for respectful behavior and provide education on the importance of maintaining an inclusive space.

Example Practice

Global Enterprises uses neutral decor in their multi-faith space and provides clear guidelines for respectful behavior. Educational sessions are held to reinforce the importance of maintaining an inclusive and respectful environment.

Conclusion

Creating spaces for multiple faith traditions is essential for fostering an inclusive and respectful workplace. By consulting with employees, designing flexible and adaptable spaces, providing essential resources, establishing guidelines for use, and encouraging participation and engagement, organizations can ensure that their multi-faith spaces meet the diverse needs of their workforce. Addressing challenges such as balancing diverse needs and maintaining neutrality and respect is crucial for creating a supportive and inclusive environment.

As we continue to explore the role of corporate chaplaincy in this book, we will delve into further strategies and best practices for addressing the common issues faced by employees. By understanding and addressing these challenges, organizations can create environments where employees feel valued, supported, and inspired.

Handling Religious Conflicts and Misunderstandings

Introduction

Religious conflicts and misunderstandings can arise in diverse workplaces, potentially disrupting harmony and productivity. As a corporate chaplain, it is crucial to address these issues with sensitivity and expertise to foster a respectful and inclusive environment. This chapter explores strategies for handling religious conflicts and misunderstandings, providing practical guidance for chaplains to navigate these complex situations effectively.

The Importance of Addressing Religious Conflicts and Misunderstandings

1. Maintaining Workplace Harmony

Definition and Importance

Addressing religious conflicts and misunderstandings is essential for maintaining a harmonious and productive workplace. Conflicts can lead to tension, reduced morale, and decreased collaboration if left unaddressed.

Impact

- Reduced Tension: Effectively addressing conflicts reduces tension and promotes a peaceful work environment.

- Increased Collaboration: Resolving misunderstandings fosters better teamwork and collaboration among employees.

- Enhanced Morale: Employees feel respected and valued, leading to higher morale and job satisfaction.

Example

At Global Enterprises, the corporate chaplain intervenes in religious conflicts, using mediation techniques to resolve issues and restore harmony, resulting in a more cohesive and collaborative work environment.

2. Promoting Inclusivity and Respect

Definition and Importance

Handling religious conflicts and misunderstandings with care promotes inclusivity and respect for diverse beliefs, ensuring that all employees feel valued.

Impact

- Inclusive Culture: Promotes an inclusive culture where diverse beliefs are respected and valued.

- Respectful Interactions: Encourages respectful interactions among employees, reducing the likelihood of future conflicts.

- Positive Reputation: Enhances the organization's reputation as a respectful and inclusive workplace.

Example

Wellness Tech Ltd. prioritizes inclusivity and respect by addressing religious conflicts promptly. This proactive approach fosters a positive workplace culture and enhances the company's reputation.

Strategies for Handling Religious Conflicts and Misunderstandings

1. Establishing Clear Policies and Guidelines

Definition and Importance

Clear policies and guidelines provide a framework for addressing religious conflicts and misunderstandings, ensuring consistency and fairness.

Implementation

- Anti-Discrimination Policies: Develop and enforce policies that prohibit discrimination and harassment based on religion.

- Conflict Resolution Procedures: Establish procedures for reporting and resolving religious conflicts, including steps for investigation and mediation.

- Guidelines for Respectful Behavior: Create guidelines that outline expected behaviors and interactions, promoting respect and inclusivity.

Example Practice

At Creative Minds Corp, the corporate chaplain collaborates with HR to develop anti-discrimination policies and conflict resolution procedures. These policies and procedures provide a clear framework for addressing religious conflicts.

2. Providing Education and Training

Definition and Importance

Education and training help employees understand and respect diverse religious beliefs, reducing the likelihood of conflicts and misunderstandings.

Implementation

- Cultural Competency Training: Offer regular cultural competency training sessions that include information on religious diversity and respectful interactions.

- Workshops and Seminars: Conduct workshops and seminars on religious diversity, conflict resolution, and effective communication.

- Resource Materials: Provide educational materials on different religions and cultural practices to promote understanding and respect.

Example Practice

Global Enterprises offers cultural competency training and workshops on religious diversity. These sessions educate employees on respectful interactions and reduce the likelihood of conflicts.

3. Mediation and Conflict Resolution

Definition and Importance

Mediation and conflict resolution involve addressing religious conflicts directly, facilitating open dialogue and finding mutually acceptable solutions.

Implementation

- Neutral Mediation: Act as a neutral mediator to facilitate discussions between conflicting parties, ensuring that all perspectives are heard and respected.

- Conflict Resolution Techniques: Use conflict resolution techniques, such as active listening, empathy, and problem-solving, to address and resolve conflicts.

- Follow-Up: Conduct follow-up meetings to ensure that the conflict has been resolved and that relationships have been restored.

Example Practice

At Wellness Tech Ltd., the corporate chaplain mediates religious conflicts by facilitating open and respectful discussions. Follow-up meetings are conducted to ensure that the resolution is effective and lasting.

4. Encouraging Open Dialogue

Definition and Importance

Encouraging open dialogue about religious beliefs and practices promotes understanding and reduces the likelihood of conflicts.

Implementation

- Interfaith Dialogues: Organize interfaith dialogue sessions where employees can share their beliefs and learn about others' traditions in a respectful environment.

- Open Forums: Hold open forums and town hall meetings to discuss religious diversity and address any concerns or misunderstandings.

- Anonymous Feedback: Provide opportunities for employees to give anonymous feedback about religious conflicts and suggest improvements.

Example Practice

Creative Minds Corp organizes monthly interfaith dialogues facilitated by the corporate chaplain. These sessions provide a platform for employees to share their beliefs and address any misunderstandings, fostering mutual respect.

5. Supporting Affected Employees

Definition and Importance

Providing support to employees affected by religious conflicts ensures their well-being and helps them feel valued and respected.

Implementation

- Counseling Services: Offer confidential counseling services to employees involved in or affected by religious conflicts.

- Peer Support Groups: Facilitate peer support groups where employees can share their experiences and find mutual support.

- Resource Provision: Provide resources, such as reading materials and external support contacts, to help employees navigate religious conflicts.

Example Practice

At Global Enterprises, the corporate chaplain offers counseling services to employees affected by religious conflicts. Peer support groups are also available, providing a safe space for sharing and support.

Challenges and Solutions in Handling Religious Conflicts

1. Balancing Diverse Needs and Perspectives

Definition and Importance

Balancing the diverse needs and perspectives of different religious groups can be challenging but is essential for effective conflict resolution.

Challenges

- Conflicting Beliefs: Different religious beliefs and practices may conflict, creating challenges in finding mutually acceptable solutions.

- Bias and Prejudice: Unconscious biases and prejudices can hinder the resolution process and exacerbate conflicts.

Solutions

- Neutral Mediation: Ensure that mediation is neutral and unbiased, respecting all perspectives and beliefs.

- Education and Awareness: Promote education and awareness to reduce biases and promote understanding and respect.

Example Practice

At Creative Minds Corp, the corporate chaplain ensures neutrality in mediation and provides bias training to reduce prejudices and promote fair conflict resolution.

2. Maintaining Confidentiality and Trust

Definition and Importance

Maintaining confidentiality and trust is crucial for effective conflict resolution and ensuring that employees feel safe to share their concerns.

Challenges

- Confidentiality Breaches: Breaches of confidentiality can undermine trust and hinder the resolution process.

- Fear of Retaliation: Employees may fear retaliation for reporting religious conflicts or participating in mediation.

Solutions

- Strict Confidentiality Policies: Implement and enforce strict confidentiality policies to protect employees' privacy.

- Non-Retaliation Policies: Develop non-retaliation policies to ensure that employees can report conflicts and participate in mediation without fear of repercussions.

Example Practice

Global Enterprises enforces strict confidentiality and non-retaliation policies, ensuring that employees feel safe and supported in reporting religious conflicts.

Conclusion

Handling religious conflicts and misunderstandings effectively is essential for maintaining a harmonious and inclusive workplace. By establishing clear policies and guidelines, providing education and training, using mediation and conflict resolution techniques, encouraging open dialogue, and supporting affected employees, corporate chaplains can navigate these complex situations with sensitivity and expertise. Addressing challenges such as balancing diverse needs and maintaining confidentiality is crucial for fostering a respectful and inclusive environment.

As we continue to explore the role of corporate chaplaincy in this book, we will delve into further strategies and best practices for addressing the common issues faced by

employees. By understanding and addressing these challenges, organizations can create environments where employees feel valued, supported, and inspired.

CHAPTER 06

LEGAL AND ETHICAL CONSIDERATIONS

Navigating Legalities

Understanding the Legal Framework for Corporate Chaplaincy

Introduction

Corporate chaplaincy involves providing spiritual and emotional support within the workplace, which raises important legal and ethical considerations. Understanding the legal framework that governs corporate chaplaincy is crucial for ensuring that chaplaincy programs comply with laws and regulations while respecting the rights and beliefs of all employees. This chapter explores the key legal aspects of corporate chaplaincy, offering guidance on navigating these complexities effectively.

The Importance of Legal Compliance in Corporate Chaplaincy

1. Ensuring Fair Treatment

Definition and Importance

Legal compliance ensures that all employees are treated fairly and that their rights are protected. It helps prevent discrimination and ensures that chaplaincy services are accessible to everyone.

Impact

- Equitable Access: Guarantees that all employees, regardless of their religious beliefs, have access to chaplaincy services.

- Non-Discrimination: Protects against discrimination based on religion, ensuring a fair and inclusive workplace.

- Legal Protection: Shields the organization from legal challenges related to religious discrimination or harassment.

Example

At Global Enterprises, the corporate chaplaincy program is designed to be inclusive and non-discriminatory, ensuring that all employees feel respected and valued.

2. Promoting Ethical Standards

Definition and Importance

Adhering to legal and ethical standards promotes trust and integrity in the chaplaincy program, ensuring that it is conducted with professionalism and respect.

Impact

- Trust and Credibility: Builds trust and credibility with employees and stakeholders.

- Professionalism: Ensures that chaplaincy services are provided ethically and professionally.

- Employee Confidence: Enhances employee confidence in the chaplaincy program and its adherence to ethical standards.

Example

Wellness Tech Ltd. maintains high ethical standards in its chaplaincy program, ensuring that all services are provided with integrity and respect for employees' rights.

Key Legal Considerations for Corporate Chaplaincy

1. Religious Accommodation

Definition and Importance

Religious accommodation involves providing reasonable adjustments to enable employees to practice their religious beliefs without undue hardship to the employer.

Implementation

- Flexible Scheduling: Offer flexible work schedules to accommodate religious observances, such as prayer times and religious holidays.

- Dress Code Adjustments: Allow adjustments to dress codes to accommodate religious attire, such as hijabs, turbans, and yarmulkes.

- Prayer and Meditation Spaces: Provide designated spaces for prayer and meditation to support employees' spiritual practices.

Example Practice

At Creative Minds Corp, the corporate chaplain works with HR to implement flexible scheduling policies and provide prayer spaces, ensuring that employees can observe their religious practices.

2. Non-Discrimination Policies

Definition and Importance

Non-discrimination policies protect employees from discrimination based on religion and ensure that all employees are treated equitably.

Implementation

- Clear Policies: Develop and communicate clear non-discrimination policies that explicitly include religion as a protected characteristic.

- Training Programs: Offer training programs to educate employees and managers about religious diversity and the importance of non-discrimination.

- Complaint Procedures: Establish procedures for reporting and addressing complaints of religious discrimination or harassment.

Example Practice

Global Enterprises has clear non-discrimination policies that include religion as a protected characteristic. Regular training programs and established complaint procedures ensure that these policies are upheld.

3. Confidentiality and Privacy

Definition and Importance

Maintaining confidentiality and privacy in chaplaincy services is crucial for protecting employees' personal information and fostering trust.

Implementation

- Confidentiality Agreements: Require chaplains to sign confidentiality agreements to protect employees' personal information.

- Secure Record Keeping: Implement secure systems for storing and managing confidential information obtained during chaplaincy sessions.

- Employee Consent: Ensure that employees give informed consent before sharing any personal information with others.

Example Practice

At Wellness Tech Ltd., chaplains sign confidentiality agreements and use secure systems to manage confidential information. Employees are informed about confidentiality practices and give consent before sharing personal details.

4. Separation of Church and State

Definition and Importance

The principle of separation of church and state requires that government and public institutions, including publicly funded organizations, remain neutral regarding religion.

Implementation

- Neutrality in Services: Ensure that chaplaincy services are provided in a manner that is neutral and inclusive of all religious beliefs.

- Inclusive Programming: Design chaplaincy programs to be inclusive and respectful of all faith traditions, avoiding the promotion of any particular religion.

- Legal Compliance: Ensure that chaplaincy services comply with laws and regulations related to the separation of church and state.

Example Practice

Creative Minds Corp, a publicly funded organization, ensures that its chaplaincy program is neutral and inclusive, providing support to employees of all religious backgrounds without promoting any particular faith.

5. Informed Consent

Definition and Importance

Informed consent involves ensuring that employees are fully informed about the nature of chaplaincy services and voluntarily agree to participate.

Implementation

- Clear Communication: Clearly communicate the purpose, scope, and confidentiality practices of chaplaincy services to employees.

- Voluntary Participation: Ensure that participation in chaplaincy services is voluntary and that employees can opt out at any time.

- Documentation: Obtain written consent from employees before providing chaplaincy services, documenting their agreement to participate.

Example Practice

At Global Enterprises, employees receive clear information about chaplaincy services and provide written consent before participating. This ensures that they are fully informed and agree to the services voluntarily.

Challenges and Solutions in Navigating Legalities

1. Balancing Religious Accommodation and Operational Needs

Definition and Importance

Balancing the need for religious accommodation with the operational needs of the organization can be challenging but is essential for maintaining fairness and productivity.

Challenges

- Operational Disruptions: Accommodating religious practices may sometimes disrupt operational processes.

- Perceived Favoritism: Providing accommodations for some employees may lead to perceptions of favoritism or unfairness among others.

Solutions

- Reasonable Accommodation: Provide reasonable accommodations that do not cause undue hardship to the organization.

- Transparent Communication: Communicate clearly with all employees about the reasons for accommodations and the organization's commitment to fairness.

Example Practice

At Creative Minds Corp, the corporate chaplain and HR collaborate to provide reasonable accommodations for religious practices while ensuring that operational needs are met. Transparent communication helps manage perceptions of favoritism.

2. Maintaining Confidentiality and Trust

Definition and Importance

Maintaining confidentiality and trust is crucial for the effectiveness of chaplaincy services and for protecting employees' personal information.

Challenges

- Confidentiality Breaches: Accidental or intentional breaches of confidentiality can undermine trust and harm employees.

- Complex Cases: Handling complex cases that require coordination with other professionals while maintaining confidentiality.

Solutions

- Strict Confidentiality Policies: Implement and enforce strict confidentiality policies to protect employees' personal information.

- Professional Coordination: Coordinate with other professionals (e.g., HR, counselors) while maintaining confidentiality through secure communication and consent procedures.

Example Practice

Global Enterprises enforces strict confidentiality policies and coordinates with other professionals using secure communication methods. Employees are informed about confidentiality practices and give consent before sharing information.

Conclusion

Understanding and navigating the legal framework for corporate chaplaincy is essential for ensuring compliance, fairness, and respect for employees' rights. By focusing on religious accommodation, non-discrimination policies, confidentiality and privacy, separation of church and state, and informed consent, chaplains can provide effective and legally compliant services. Addressing challenges such as balancing religious accommodation with operational needs and maintaining confidentiality is crucial for fostering a supportive and inclusive workplace.

As we continue to explore the role of corporate chaplaincy in this book, we will delve into further strategies and best practices for addressing the common issues faced by employees. By understanding and addressing these challenges, organizations can create environments where employees feel valued, supported, and inspired.

Employee Rights and Protections

Introduction

In the realm of corporate chaplaincy, understanding and upholding employee rights and protections is essential. Ensuring that employees' rights are respected not only fosters trust and respect but also ensures compliance with legal standards. This chapter outlines the key employee rights and protections relevant to corporate chaplaincy, providing guidance on how to navigate these important issues effectively.

The Importance of Upholding Employee Rights

1. Fostering Trust and Respect

Definition and Importance

Respecting employee rights fosters a culture of trust and respect within the workplace. When employees feel their rights are protected, they are more likely to engage fully and positively in their work.

Impact

- Enhanced Trust: Builds trust between employees and the organization.

- Higher Engagement: Leads to greater employee engagement and job satisfaction.

- Positive Culture: Contributes to a positive and respectful workplace culture.

Example

At Global Enterprises, the corporate chaplaincy program emphasizes respecting employee rights, which has led to a more engaged and trusting workforce.

2. Ensuring Legal Compliance

Definition and Importance

Upholding employee rights ensures that the organization complies with relevant laws and regulations, protecting it from legal challenges and fostering a fair workplace.

Impact

- Legal Protection: Protects the organization from potential legal issues related to violations of employee rights.

- Fair Treatment: Ensures fair treatment of all employees, promoting equity and justice.

- Reputation Management: Enhances the organization's reputation as a fair and ethical employer.

Example

Wellness Tech Ltd. ensures that its corporate chaplaincy program adheres to all relevant laws and regulations, maintaining legal compliance and promoting fair treatment of employees.

Key Employee Rights and Protections

1. Freedom of Religion

Definition and Importance

Employees have the right to practice their religion freely and without discrimination in the workplace. This right is protected by laws such as the Civil Rights Act in the United States.

Implementation

- Anti-Discrimination Policies: Develop and enforce policies that prohibit discrimination based on religion.

- Accommodations for Religious Practices: Provide reasonable accommodations for religious practices, such as prayer times, religious attire, and observance of religious holidays.

- Training and Awareness: Offer training to employees and managers on religious diversity and the importance of respecting freedom of religion.

Example Practice

At Creative Minds Corp, the corporate chaplain works with HR to develop anti-discrimination policies and provide accommodations for religious practices, ensuring that all employees can practice their religion freely.

2. Privacy and Confidentiality

Definition and Importance

Employees have the right to privacy and confidentiality, particularly regarding personal information shared in chaplaincy sessions. Maintaining confidentiality is essential for building trust.

Implementation

- Confidentiality Policies: Implement strict confidentiality policies to protect employees' personal information.

- Secure Record Keeping: Use secure systems for storing and managing confidential information obtained during chaplaincy sessions.

- Informed Consent: Ensure that employees provide informed consent before any personal information is shared with others.

Example Practice

Wellness Tech Ltd. enforces strict confidentiality policies and uses secure systems to manage confidential information. Employees provide informed consent before sharing personal details, ensuring their privacy is protected.

3. Equal Opportunity and Non-Discrimination

Definition and Importance

Employees have the right to equal opportunity and non-discrimination in all aspects of employment, including access to chaplaincy services. This is protected by various anti-discrimination laws.

Implementation

- Equal Access: Ensure that all employees have equal access to chaplaincy services, regardless of their religion or belief system.

- Non-Discrimination Training: Provide training on non-discrimination and equal opportunity to all employees and managers.

- Reporting Mechanisms: Establish mechanisms for reporting and addressing complaints of discrimination or unequal treatment.

Example Practice

At Global Enterprises, all employees have equal access to chaplaincy services, and the organization provides regular non-discrimination training. Reporting mechanisms are in place to address any complaints promptly.

4. Right to Refuse Participation

Definition and Importance

Employees have the right to refuse participation in any religious or spiritual activities, including those offered by the chaplaincy program, without fear of retaliation or discrimination.

Implementation

- Voluntary Participation: Ensure that participation in chaplaincy services is entirely voluntary and that employees can opt-out at any time.

- Clear Communication: Communicate clearly to employees that they have the right to refuse participation without any negative consequences.

- Non-Retaliation Policies: Implement policies that protect employees from retaliation if they choose not to participate in chaplaincy services.

Example Practice

Creative Minds Corp ensures that all chaplaincy services are voluntary and clearly communicates this to employees. Non-retaliation policies protect employees who choose not to participate.

5. Access to Reasonable Accommodations

Definition and Importance

Employees have the right to reasonable accommodations for their religious practices, as long as these accommodations do not cause undue hardship to the employer.

Implementation

- Accommodation Requests: Develop a process for employees to request religious accommodations, such as time off for religious holidays or adjustments to work schedules.

- Review and Approval: Establish a fair and consistent process for reviewing and approving accommodation requests.

- Monitoring and Feedback: Monitor the effectiveness of accommodations and gather feedback from employees to make necessary adjustments.

Example Practice

At Wellness Tech Ltd., employees can request religious accommodations through a straightforward process. The corporate chaplain and HR review and approve requests fairly and consistently, ensuring that employees can practice their religion.

Challenges and Solutions in Upholding Employee Rights

1. Balancing Rights and Operational Needs

Definition and Importance

Balancing employees' rights with operational needs can be challenging but is essential for maintaining fairness and productivity.

Challenges

- Operational Disruptions: Accommodating religious practices may sometimes disrupt operational processes.

- Perceived Unfairness: Providing accommodations for some employees may lead to perceptions of unfairness among others.

Solutions

- Reasonable Accommodation: Provide reasonable accommodations that do not cause undue hardship to the organization.

- Transparent Communication: Communicate clearly with all employees about the reasons for accommodations and the organization's commitment to fairness.

Example Practice

At Creative Minds Corp, the corporate chaplain and HR collaborate to balance religious accommodations with operational needs, ensuring fairness and productivity.

2. Maintaining Confidentiality in Complex Cases

Definition and Importance

Maintaining confidentiality in complex cases that require coordination with other professionals is crucial for protecting employees' privacy.

Challenges

- Confidentiality Breaches: Accidental or intentional breaches of confidentiality can undermine trust and harm employees.

- Complex Coordination: Handling complex cases while maintaining confidentiality can be challenging.

Solutions

- Strict Confidentiality Policies: Implement and enforce strict confidentiality policies to protect employees' personal information.

- Secure Coordination: Coordinate with other professionals (e.g., HR, counselors) using secure communication methods and obtaining employee consent.

Example Practice

Global Enterprises enforces strict confidentiality policies and coordinates complex cases securely, ensuring that employees' privacy is protected.

Conclusion

Upholding employee rights and protections is fundamental to the success of corporate chaplaincy programs. By focusing on freedom of religion, privacy and confidentiality, equal opportunity and non-discrimination, the right to refuse participation, and access to reasonable accommodations, chaplains can ensure that all employees feel respected and valued. Addressing challenges such as balancing rights with operational needs and maintaining confidentiality in complex cases is crucial for fostering a supportive and inclusive workplace.

As we continue to explore the role of corporate chaplaincy in this book, we will delve into further strategies and best practices for addressing the common issues faced by employees. By understanding and addressing these challenges, organizations can create environments where employees feel valued, supported, and inspired.

Company Policies and Compliance

Introduction

Establishing and adhering to comprehensive company policies is crucial for ensuring legal compliance and promoting an ethical, respectful workplace. For corporate chaplaincy programs, clear policies provide guidance and structure, ensuring that services are provided consistently and fairly. This chapter outlines key considerations for developing and maintaining effective company policies related to corporate chaplaincy and compliance.

The Importance of Clear Company Policies

1. Ensuring Consistency and Fairness

Definition and Importance

Clear policies ensure that chaplaincy services are delivered consistently and fairly across the organization, providing a reliable framework for decision-making and behavior.

Impact

- Uniform Standards: Establishes uniform standards for the provision of chaplaincy services.

- Fair Treatment: Ensures that all employees are treated fairly and equitably.

- Reduced Conflicts: Minimizes misunderstandings and conflicts by providing clear guidelines.

Example

At Global Enterprises, the corporate chaplaincy program operates under well-defined policies, ensuring consistent and fair treatment of all employees.

2. Facilitating Legal Compliance

Definition and Importance

Comprehensive policies help ensure that the organization complies with relevant laws and regulations, reducing the risk of legal issues and fostering a lawful workplace environment.

Impact

- Legal Protection: Protects the organization from potential legal challenges related to violations of employee rights.

- Ethical Standards: Promotes adherence to high ethical standards in the provision of chaplaincy services.

- Regulatory Compliance: Ensures compliance with employment laws and regulations, such as those related to discrimination, privacy, and accommodation.

Example

Wellness Tech Ltd. develops policies that comply with all relevant laws and regulations, maintaining a lawful and ethical workplace environment.

Key Components of Effective Company Policies

1. Non-Discrimination and Equal Opportunity

Definition and Importance

Policies that prohibit discrimination and promote equal opportunity are fundamental to fostering an inclusive and fair workplace.

Implementation

- Policy Development: Create comprehensive non-discrimination and equal opportunity policies that explicitly include religion as a protected characteristic.

- Training Programs: Provide regular training on non-discrimination and equal opportunity for all employees and managers.

- Complaint Procedures: Establish clear procedures for reporting and addressing complaints of discrimination or unequal treatment.

Example Practice

At Creative Minds Corp, the corporate chaplain and HR develop and enforce non-discrimination and equal opportunity policies. Training programs and complaint procedures ensure that these policies are upheld.

2. Religious Accommodation

Definition and Importance

Policies that address religious accommodation ensure that employees can practice their religion freely while balancing the operational needs of the organization.

Implementation

- Accommodation Requests: Develop a process for employees to request religious accommodations, such as time off for religious holidays or adjustments to work schedules.

- Review Process: Establish a fair and consistent process for reviewing and approving accommodation requests.

- Monitoring and Feedback: Continuously monitor the effectiveness of accommodations and gather feedback from employees to make necessary adjustments.

Example Practice

Global Enterprises implements a straightforward process for requesting religious accommodations. The corporate chaplain and HR review requests fairly and ensure that accommodations meet employees' needs without disrupting operations.

3. Confidentiality and Privacy

Definition and Importance

Policies that protect confidentiality and privacy are crucial for maintaining trust and ensuring that personal information is handled appropriately.

Implementation

- Confidentiality Agreements: Require chaplains and relevant staff to sign confidentiality agreements.

- Secure Systems: Implement secure systems for storing and managing confidential information obtained during chaplaincy sessions.

- Informed Consent: Ensure that employees provide informed consent before any personal information is shared with others.

Example Practice

Wellness Tech Ltd. enforces confidentiality agreements and uses secure systems for managing confidential information. Employees provide informed consent, ensuring their privacy is protected.

4. Voluntary Participation

Definition and Importance

Policies that ensure participation in chaplaincy services are voluntary protect employees' rights and foster a respectful and inclusive environment.

Implementation

- Clear Communication: Communicate clearly to employees that participation in chaplaincy services is voluntary and that they can opt-out at any time.

- Non-Retaliation Policies: Implement policies that protect employees from retaliation if they choose not to participate in chaplaincy services.

- Feedback Mechanisms: Provide mechanisms for employees to give feedback on chaplaincy services, ensuring that their participation remains voluntary and respectful.

Example Practice

At Creative Minds Corp, participation in chaplaincy services is voluntary, and this is clearly communicated to all employees. Non-retaliation policies protect employees who choose not to participate.

5. Training and Awareness

Definition and Importance

Training and awareness programs ensure that all employees understand the company policies related to chaplaincy and compliance, fostering a culture of respect and inclusion.

Implementation

- Regular Training: Provide regular training on company policies, including non-discrimination, confidentiality, religious accommodation, and voluntary participation.

- Awareness Campaigns: Conduct awareness campaigns to highlight the importance of these policies and ensure that all employees are informed.

- Policy Accessibility: Make company policies easily accessible to all employees, both online and in physical formats.

Example Practice

Global Enterprises provides regular training on company policies and conducts awareness campaigns to ensure that all employees are informed and understand the importance of these policies.

Challenges and Solutions in Implementing Policies

1. Balancing Flexibility and Consistency

Definition and Importance

Balancing the need for flexibility with the need for consistency in policy implementation can be challenging but is essential for fair and effective management.

Challenges

- Operational Needs: Balancing religious accommodations with operational needs can be difficult.

- Perceived Unfairness: Ensuring that policies are applied consistently to avoid perceptions of unfairness.

Solutions

- Reasonable Accommodation: Provide accommodations that do not cause undue hardship to the organization.

- Transparent Communication: Clearly communicate the reasons for accommodations and the organization's commitment to fairness and consistency.

Example Practice

At Creative Minds Corp, the corporate chaplain and HR work together to balance religious accommodations with operational needs, ensuring fair and consistent policy implementation.

2. Maintaining Policy Relevance

Definition and Importance

Policies must remain relevant and effective as organizational needs and legal requirements evolve.

Challenges

- Changing Regulations: Keeping up with changing laws and regulations.

- Evolving Workforce Needs: Adapting policies to meet the evolving needs of a diverse workforce.

Solutions

- Regular Reviews: Conduct regular reviews of company policies to ensure they remain current and effective.

- Employee Feedback: Gather feedback from employees to understand their needs and make necessary policy adjustments.

Example Practice

Global Enterprises conducts annual reviews of its policies and gathers employee feedback to ensure that policies remain relevant and effective.

Conclusion

Developing and maintaining comprehensive company policies is crucial for ensuring legal compliance and promoting an ethical, respectful workplace. By focusing on non-discrimination and equal opportunity, religious accommodation, confidentiality and privacy, voluntary participation, and training and awareness, organizations can create a supportive and inclusive environment. Addressing challenges such as balancing flexibility with consistency and maintaining policy relevance is essential for effective policy implementation.

As we continue to explore the role of corporate chaplaincy in this book, we will delve into further strategies and best practices for addressing the common issues faced by employees. By understanding and addressing these challenges, organizations can create environments where employees feel valued, supported, and inspired.

Maintaining Ethical Standards

Confidentiality and Trust

Introduction

Confidentiality and trust are fundamental to the practice of corporate chaplaincy. They are essential for building effective relationships with employees and ensuring that chaplaincy services are provided with integrity and respect. This chapter explores the importance of maintaining confidentiality and trust, providing strategies for chaplains to uphold these ethical standards effectively.

The Importance of Confidentiality and Trust

1. Building Effective Relationships

Definition and Importance

Confidentiality involves protecting the privacy of personal information shared by employees, while trust is the foundation of any supportive relationship. Together, they enable chaplains to build effective, supportive relationships with employees.

Impact

- Open Communication: Encourages employees to communicate openly and honestly with chaplains.

- Emotional Safety: Creates a safe environment where employees feel emotionally secure.

- Stronger Support: Enhances the effectiveness of chaplaincy services by fostering deeper connections and trust.

Example

At Global Enterprises, the corporate chaplain maintains strict confidentiality, ensuring that employees feel safe to share their concerns, which leads to more effective support and stronger relationships.

2. Ensuring Ethical Integrity

Definition and Importance

Maintaining confidentiality and trust is essential for upholding ethical integrity in chaplaincy services. It demonstrates a commitment to professional standards and ethical behavior.

Impact

- Professionalism: Enhances the professionalism and credibility of chaplaincy services.

- Ethical Compliance: Ensures compliance with ethical guidelines and legal requirements related to confidentiality.

- Employee Confidence: Increases employee confidence in the chaplaincy program and its commitment to ethical standards.

Example

Wellness Tech Ltd. emphasizes ethical integrity in its chaplaincy program, maintaining confidentiality and trust to uphold professional standards and employee confidence.

Key Strategies for Maintaining Confidentiality and Trust

1. Establishing Clear Confidentiality Policies

Definition and Importance

Clear confidentiality policies provide a framework for protecting personal information and maintaining trust.

Implementation

- Policy Development: Develop comprehensive confidentiality policies that outline the protection of personal information and the circumstances under which information may be disclosed.

- Employee Communication: Clearly communicate confidentiality policies to all employees, ensuring they understand their rights and the protection measures in place.

- Regular Reviews: Conduct regular reviews of confidentiality policies to ensure they remain current and effective.

Example Practice

At Creative Minds Corp, the corporate chaplain and HR develop clear confidentiality policies and communicate them to employees. Regular reviews ensure that these policies remain effective and relevant.

2. Training and Education

Definition and Importance

Training and education ensure that chaplains and relevant staff understand and adhere to confidentiality policies and ethical standards.

Implementation

- Chaplains Training: Provide comprehensive training for chaplains on confidentiality policies, ethical standards, and best practices for maintaining trust.

- Ongoing Education: Offer ongoing education and refresher courses to keep chaplains updated on changes in policies and ethical guidelines.

- Awareness Programs: Implement awareness programs for all employees to reinforce the importance of confidentiality and trust in chaplaincy services.

Example Practice

Global Enterprises provides regular training for chaplains on confidentiality and ethical standards, along with awareness programs for all employees to reinforce the importance of these principles.

3. Secure Handling of Information

Definition and Importance

Secure handling of personal information is critical for maintaining confidentiality and trust.

Implementation

- Secure Storage Systems: Use secure systems for storing and managing confidential information obtained during chaplaincy sessions, such as encrypted digital files and locked physical storage.

- Access Control: Implement strict access control measures to ensure that only authorized personnel have access to confidential information.

- Data Protection Practices: Follow best practices for data protection, including regular audits, secure communication channels, and compliance with data protection regulations.

Example Practice

At Wellness Tech Ltd., confidential information is stored in encrypted digital files and locked physical storage. Access is strictly controlled, and regular audits ensure compliance with data protection practices.

4. Obtaining Informed Consent

Definition and Importance

Informed consent involves ensuring that employees understand and agree to the terms of confidentiality before sharing personal information.

Implementation

- Clear Communication: Clearly explain the confidentiality policies and any potential limitations to employees before starting chaplaincy sessions.

- Written Consent: Obtain written consent from employees, documenting their agreement to the confidentiality terms.

- Voluntary Participation: Ensure that participation in chaplaincy services is voluntary and that employees can withdraw their consent at any time.

Example Practice

At Creative Minds Corp, the corporate chaplain obtains written consent from employees before chaplaincy sessions, clearly explaining confidentiality policies and ensuring voluntary participation.

5. Regular Supervision and Support

Definition and Importance

Regular supervision and support for chaplains help maintain high ethical standards and address any challenges related to confidentiality and trust.

Implementation

- Supervision Meetings: Hold regular supervision meetings for chaplains to discuss ethical challenges, receive guidance, and ensure adherence to confidentiality policies.

- Peer Support Groups: Establish peer support groups for chaplains to share experiences, provide mutual support, and reinforce ethical practices.

- Continuous Improvement: Encourage continuous improvement by regularly reviewing and updating confidentiality practices based on feedback and new developments.

Example Practice

Global Enterprises holds regular supervision meetings for chaplains and facilitates peer support groups, ensuring continuous adherence to ethical standards and confidentiality practices.

Challenges and Solutions in Maintaining Confidentiality and Trust

1. Balancing Confidentiality with Duty of Care

Definition and Importance

Balancing the need to maintain confidentiality with the duty of care, such as reporting imminent harm, can be challenging but is essential for ethical chaplaincy.

Challenges

- Imminent Harm: Situations where an employee poses a risk of harm to themselves or others may require breaching confidentiality.

- Legal Obligations: Legal obligations, such as mandatory reporting requirements, may necessitate disclosure of confidential information.

Solutions

- Clear Policies: Develop clear policies outlining the circumstances under which confidentiality may be breached and the procedures for doing so.

- Training and Guidance: Provide training and guidance to chaplains on balancing confidentiality with duty of care and legal obligations.

- Employee Communication: Communicate potential limitations of confidentiality to employees, ensuring they understand the circumstances under which information may be disclosed.

Example Practice

At Creative Minds Corp, the corporate chaplain and HR develop policies for handling situations involving imminent harm and legal obligations. Chaplains receive training on these policies and communicate potential limitations to employees.

2. Maintaining Confidentiality in Group Settings

Definition and Importance

Maintaining confidentiality in group settings, such as support groups or workshops, is essential for protecting participants' privacy.

Challenges

- Group Dynamics: Ensuring that all participants understand and adhere to confidentiality agreements.

- Information Sharing: Managing the sharing of personal information in a group setting.

Solutions

- Confidentiality Agreements: Require participants to sign confidentiality agreements before joining group sessions.

- Facilitator Training: Train group facilitators on managing confidentiality and handling breaches appropriately.

- Clear Guidelines: Establish clear guidelines for group sessions, outlining expectations for confidentiality and respectful behavior.

Example Practice

Global Enterprises requires participants in support groups to sign confidentiality agreements and provides training for facilitators. Clear guidelines are established to ensure confidentiality and respect in group settings.

Conclusion

Maintaining confidentiality and trust is fundamental to the effectiveness and ethical integrity of corporate chaplaincy services. By establishing clear confidentiality policies, providing training and education, securely handling information, obtaining informed consent, and offering regular supervision and support, chaplains can uphold these essential ethical standards. Addressing challenges such as balancing confidentiality with duty of care and maintaining confidentiality in group settings is crucial for fostering a supportive and respectful workplace.

As we continue to explore the role of corporate chaplaincy in this book, we will delve into further strategies and best practices for addressing the common issues faced by employees. By understanding and addressing these challenges, organizations can create environments where employees feel valued, supported, and inspired.

Ethical Dilemmas and Decision-Making

Introduction

Corporate chaplains often face ethical dilemmas that require careful consideration and sound judgment. Navigating these dilemmas is essential for maintaining the integrity and effectiveness of chaplaincy services. This chapter explores common ethical dilemmas faced by corporate chaplains and provides a framework for ethical decision-making.

The Importance of Ethical Decision-Making

1. Maintaining Professional Integrity

Definition and Importance

Professional integrity involves adhering to ethical standards and principles, even in challenging situations. It is fundamental to the credibility and trustworthiness of chaplaincy services.

Impact

- Trust and Credibility: Builds trust and credibility with employees and stakeholders.

- Consistency: Ensures consistent adherence to ethical standards, reinforcing the chaplaincy program's reliability.

- Professionalism: Enhances the overall professionalism of the chaplaincy services.

Example

At Global Enterprises, the corporate chaplain maintains professional integrity by adhering to ethical guidelines, ensuring that employees trust and respect the chaplaincy services.

2. Promoting Fairness and Respect

Definition and Importance

Ethical decision-making promotes fairness and respect for all individuals, ensuring that their rights and dignity are upheld.

Impact

- Fair Treatment: Ensures that all employees are treated fairly and with respect.

- Equity: Promotes equity by considering the needs and circumstances of all individuals.

- Respect for Rights: Upholds the rights and dignity of employees, fostering a respectful workplace culture.

Example

Wellness Tech Ltd. emphasizes fairness and respect in its chaplaincy program, ensuring that all employees are treated equitably and their rights are respected.

Common Ethical Dilemmas Faced by Corporate Chaplains

1. Confidentiality vs. Duty to Report

Definition and Importance

Balancing the need to maintain confidentiality with the duty to report issues such as harm or legal violations is a common ethical dilemma.

Scenario

An employee confides in the chaplain about experiencing domestic violence but requests that the information be kept confidential. The chaplain must decide whether to respect the employee's request or report the situation to ensure the employee's safety.

Decision-Making Framework

- Assess the Risk: Evaluate the risk of harm to the employee or others.

- Legal Obligations: Consider any legal obligations to report the situation.

- Employee Consent: Seek the employee's consent for reporting, if possible.

- Ethical Principles: Balance the principles of confidentiality and duty of care.

Example Practice

At Creative Minds Corp, the corporate chaplain assesses the risk and legal obligations, seeks the employee's consent, and balances ethical principles to make an informed decision.

2. Neutrality vs. Advocacy

Definition and Importance

Chaplains must balance the need to remain neutral with the need to advocate for employees' rights and well-being.

Scenario

An employee reports workplace harassment to the chaplain, seeking support. The chaplain must decide whether to maintain neutrality or advocate on the employee's behalf.

Decision-Making Framework

- Understand the Context: Gather comprehensive information about the situation.

- Evaluate the Impact: Assess the potential impact of maintaining neutrality vs. advocacy.

- Consult Policies: Review company policies on harassment and advocacy.

- Ethical Principles: Balance the principles of neutrality and the duty to support employee well-being.

Example Practice

At Global Enterprises, the corporate chaplain gathers information, evaluates the impact, consults policies, and balances ethical principles to determine the appropriate course of action.

3. Personal Beliefs vs. Professional Responsibility

Definition and Importance

Chaplains may face dilemmas when their personal beliefs conflict with their professional responsibilities to provide inclusive support.

Scenario

A chaplain's personal beliefs about a particular lifestyle conflict with providing support to an employee who seeks guidance on that lifestyle.

Decision-Making Framework

- Separate Personal Beliefs: Recognize and set aside personal beliefs in professional interactions.

- Focus on Professional Ethics: Adhere to professional ethical standards of inclusivity and respect.

- Seek Support: Consult with a supervisor or peer support group for guidance.

- Provide Inclusive Care: Ensure that the support provided is inclusive and respectful of the employee's beliefs and choices.

Example Practice

At Wellness Tech Ltd., the corporate chaplain sets aside personal beliefs, adheres to professional ethics, seeks support if needed, and provides inclusive care to all employees.

Framework for Ethical Decision-Making

1. Identify the Ethical Dilemma

Definition and Importance

Identifying the ethical dilemma involves recognizing the conflicting values or principles at play in a given situation.

Implementation

- Clarify the Conflict: Clearly define the conflicting values or principles.

- Gather Information: Collect all relevant information about the situation.

- Consult Ethical Guidelines: Refer to professional ethical guidelines and company policies.

Example Practice

At Creative Minds Corp, the corporate chaplain identifies the ethical dilemma, clarifies the conflict, gathers information, and consults ethical guidelines to understand the situation fully.

2. Evaluate the Options

Definition and Importance

Evaluating the options involves considering the potential actions and their consequences.

Implementation

- List Potential Actions: Identify all possible courses of action.

- Assess Consequences: Evaluate the potential consequences of each action for all parties involved.

- Weigh Ethical Principles: Consider the ethical principles that support each option.

Example Practice

Global Enterprises' corporate chaplain lists potential actions, assesses their consequences, and weighs ethical principles to evaluate the options thoroughly.

3. Make a Decision

Definition and Importance

Making a decision involves selecting the best course of action based on the evaluation of options and ethical principles.

Implementation

- Balance Principles: Balance the ethical principles and values involved.

- Seek Input: Consult with supervisors, colleagues, or ethical advisors if needed.

- Commit to Action: Make a decision and commit to the chosen course of action.

Example Practice

At Wellness Tech Ltd., the corporate chaplain balances ethical principles, seeks input if needed, and commits to the best course of action.

4. Implement the Decision

Definition and Importance

Implementing the decision involves taking the necessary steps to carry out the chosen course of action.

Implementation

- Plan the Implementation: Develop a clear plan for implementing the decision.

- Communicate Clearly: Communicate the decision and its rationale to relevant parties.

- Follow Through: Ensure that the decision is implemented effectively and follow through on any necessary actions.

Example Practice

At Creative Minds Corp, the corporate chaplain develops a clear implementation plan, communicates the decision clearly, and follows through to ensure effective implementation.

5. Reflect and Learn

Definition and Importance

Reflecting and learning from the decision-making process helps improve future ethical decision-making and professional practice.

Implementation

- Evaluate the Outcome: Assess the outcomes of the decision and its impact on all parties involved.

- Reflect on the Process: Reflect on the decision-making process and identify any lessons learned.

- Seek Feedback: Obtain feedback from supervisors, colleagues, or employees to gain different perspectives.

- Document Insights: Document insights and lessons learned to inform future practice.

Example Practice

Global Enterprises' corporate chaplain evaluates the outcomes, reflects on the process, seeks feedback, and documents insights to continuously improve ethical decision-making.

Conclusion

Navigating ethical dilemmas is a critical aspect of corporate chaplaincy. By identifying ethical dilemmas, evaluating options, making informed decisions, implementing those decisions effectively, and reflecting on the outcomes, chaplains can uphold high ethical standards and maintain professional integrity. Addressing common ethical dilemmas such as confidentiality vs. duty to report, neutrality vs. advocacy, and personal beliefs vs. professional responsibility is essential for providing effective and ethical chaplaincy services.

As we continue to explore the role of corporate chaplaincy in this book, we will delve into further strategies and best practices for addressing the common issues faced by employees. By understanding and addressing these challenges, organizations can create environments where employees feel valued, supported, and inspired.

Continuous Professional Development

Introduction

Continuous professional development is crucial for corporate chaplains to maintain their effectiveness, stay updated with current best practices, and uphold ethical standards. This chapter explores the importance of ongoing education and development for chaplains, outlining strategies to ensure continuous professional growth.

The Importance of Continuous Professional Development

1. Maintaining Competence and Skills

Definition and Importance

Continuous professional development ensures that chaplains maintain and enhance their skills and knowledge, staying competent in their roles.

Impact

- Up-to-Date Knowledge: Keeps chaplains informed about the latest developments in their field.

- Skill Enhancement: Allows chaplains to develop new skills and refine existing ones.

- Professional Competence: Ensures that chaplains remain competent and effective in their roles.

Example

At Global Enterprises, the corporate chaplain regularly participates in professional development programs to stay updated with the latest best practices and enhance their skills.

2. Upholding Ethical Standards

Definition and Importance

Ongoing professional development helps chaplains uphold ethical standards by providing them with the knowledge and tools to navigate ethical dilemmas effectively.

Impact

- Ethical Awareness: Increases awareness of ethical issues and how to address them.

- Best Practices: Promotes adherence to best practices and ethical guidelines.

- Professional Integrity: Enhances the integrity and credibility of chaplaincy services.

Example

Wellness Tech Ltd. emphasizes the importance of professional development for its chaplains, ensuring they are well-versed in ethical standards and best practices.

Strategies for Continuous Professional Development

1. Regular Training and Workshops

Definition and Importance

Regular training and workshops provide opportunities for chaplains to learn new skills, update their knowledge, and stay informed about industry trends.

Implementation

- Scheduled Training: Organize regular training sessions on various topics relevant to chaplaincy, such as counseling techniques, ethical decision-making, and cultural competency.

- Interactive Workshops: Conduct interactive workshops that encourage active participation and hands-on learning.

- Expert Instructors: Engage expert instructors and industry leaders to deliver training sessions and workshops.

Example Practice

At Creative Minds Corp, the corporate chaplain participates in monthly training sessions and workshops, learning from experts and peers to stay current and effective in their role.

2. Continuing Education Programs

Definition and Importance

Continuing education programs, such as courses and certifications, provide structured learning opportunities for chaplains to deepen their knowledge and skills.

Implementation

- Accredited Courses: Enroll in accredited courses and certification programs that offer in-depth knowledge and specialized training.

- Online Learning: Utilize online learning platforms to access courses and training programs that can be completed at their own pace.

- Professional Development Credits: Earn professional development credits through continuing education programs, contributing to career advancement.

Example Practice

Global Enterprises supports its chaplain in enrolling in continuing education programs, allowing them to earn certifications and enhance their professional credentials.

3. Professional Associations and Networks

Definition and Importance

Joining professional associations and networks provides chaplains with access to resources, support, and opportunities for collaboration and learning.

Implementation

- Membership in Associations: Join professional associations related to chaplaincy, such as the Association of Professional Chaplains (APC) or the National Association of Catholic Chaplains (NACC).

- Networking Opportunities: Participate in networking events, conferences, and seminars to connect with other professionals in the field.

- Resource Access: Utilize resources and publications offered by professional associations to stay informed about industry trends and best practices.

Example Practice

Wellness Tech Ltd.'s corporate chaplain is a member of several professional associations, participating in conferences and accessing resources to stay updated and connected.

4. Supervision and Mentorship

Definition and Importance

Regular supervision and mentorship provide chaplains with guidance, support, and opportunities for reflective practice, enhancing their professional growth.

Implementation

- Supervision Sessions: Schedule regular supervision sessions with experienced supervisors to discuss challenges, reflect on practice, and receive constructive feedback.

- Mentorship Programs: Engage in mentorship programs where experienced chaplains mentor less experienced ones, providing guidance and support.

- Peer Support Groups: Participate in peer support groups where chaplains can share experiences, discuss challenges, and learn from each other.

Example Practice

At Creative Minds Corp, the corporate chaplain participates in regular supervision sessions and mentorship programs, benefiting from the guidance and support of experienced professionals.

5. Self-Directed Learning

Definition and Importance

Self-diected learning involves taking personal initiative to pursue knowledge and skills development through various resources and activities.

Implementation

- Reading and Research: Regularly read books, articles, and research papers related to chaplaincy, ethics, and related fields.

- Online Resources: Utilize online resources such as webinars, podcasts, and professional forums to learn about new developments and best practices.

- Reflective Practice: Engage in reflective practice by keeping a journal, reflecting on experiences, and identifying areas for improvement.

Example Practice

Global Enterprises' corporate chaplain dedicates time to self-directed learning, reading relevant literature and engaging in reflective practice to enhance their professional development.

Challenges and Solutions in Continuous Professional Development

1. Balancing Professional Development with Work Responsibilities

Definition and Importance

Balancing the demands of professional development with work responsibilities can be challenging but is essential for ongoing growth.

Challenges

- Time Constraints: Finding time for professional development amidst work responsibilities.

- Resource Limitations: Limited access to resources and funding for professional development activities.

Solutions

- Scheduled Development Time: Allocate specific times for professional development activities within the work schedule.

- Employer Support: Seek support from the employer for funding and access to professional development resources.

- Efficient Learning: Utilize efficient learning methods, such as online courses and short workshops, to balance with work responsibilities.

Example Practice

At Creative Minds Corp, the corporate chaplain's work schedule includes allocated time for professional development activities, ensuring a balance between learning and work responsibilities.

2. Staying Motivated and Engaged

Definition and Importance

Maintaining motivation and engagement in continuous professional development is crucial for sustained growth and improvement.

Challenges

- Burnout: Risk of burnout due to the demands of continuous learning and work.

- Loss of Interest: Potential loss of interest in professional development activities over time.

Solutions

- Varied Learning Activities: Engage in a variety of learning activities to maintain interest and motivation.

- Goal Setting: Set clear, achievable goals for professional development to stay focused and motivated.

- Peer Encouragement: Participate in peer support groups and networks to stay motivated and inspired by others.

Example Practice

Global Enterprises' corporate chaplain sets clear professional development goals and participates in a variety of learning activities to stay motivated and engaged.

Conclusion

Continuous professional development is essential for corporate chaplains to maintain competence, uphold ethical standards, and provide effective support to employees. By engaging in regular training and workshops, continuing education programs, professional associations and networks, supervision and mentorship, and self-directed learning, chaplains can ensure their ongoing growth and effectiveness. Addressing challenges such as balancing professional development with work responsibilities and staying motivated is crucial for sustaining continuous learning and improvement.

As we continue to explore the role of corporate chaplaincy in this book, we will delve into further strategies and best practices for addressing the common issues faced by employees. By understanding and addressing these challenges, organizations can create environments where employees feel valued, supported, and inspired.

CHAPTER 07

MEASURING THE IMPACT OF CHAPLAINCY

Assessing Spiritual Programs

Introduction

Measuring the impact of corporate chaplaincy services is essential for understanding their effectiveness and value within the organization. Assessing spiritual programs involves evaluating how well these services meet the needs of employees and contribute to overall well-being and workplace culture. This chapter outlines methods for evaluating the effectiveness of chaplaincy services, providing a framework for continuous improvement.

The Importance of Evaluating Chaplaincy Services

1. Understanding Impact and Value

Definition and Importance

Evaluating chaplaincy services helps to understand their impact on employee well-being and the overall value they bring to the organization.

Impact

- Informed Decision-Making: Provides data to inform decisions about program development and resource allocation.

- Demonstrating Value: Highlights the benefits of chaplaincy services to stakeholders, justifying their existence and funding.

- Continuous Improvement: Identifies areas for improvement, leading to more effective and responsive chaplaincy services.

Example

At Global Enterprises, regular evaluation of chaplaincy services has shown significant improvements in employee well-being and job satisfaction, demonstrating the program's value to the organization.

2. Enhancing Service Delivery

Definition and Importance

Evaluating chaplaincy services ensures that they are delivered effectively and meet the diverse needs of employees.

Impact

- Tailored Support: Allows for the customization of services to better meet employee needs.

- Quality Assurance: Ensures that services are delivered to a high standard and continuously improved.

- Employee Feedback: Incorporates employee feedback into service development, enhancing relevance and responsiveness.

Example

Wellness Tech Ltd. uses evaluation data to tailor chaplaincy services to specific employee needs, enhancing the quality and effectiveness of support provided.

Methods for Evaluating the Effectiveness of Chaplaincy Services

1. Surveys and Questionnaires

Definition and Importance

Surveys and questionnaires are effective tools for collecting feedback from employees about their experiences with chaplaincy services.

Implementation

- Design: Develop surveys and questionnaires that cover key aspects of chaplaincy services, such as accessibility, quality, and impact.

- Distribution: Distribute surveys to employees through various channels, such as email, intranet, or during company meetings.

- Analysis: Analyze survey responses to identify trends, strengths, and areas for improvement.

Example Practice

At Creative Minds Corp, the corporate chaplain distributes annual surveys to gather feedback from employees about their experiences with chaplaincy services. The data collected is used to make informed improvements to the program.

2. Focus Groups and Interviews

Definition and Importance

Focus groups and interviews provide in-depth insights into employee experiences and perceptions of chaplaincy services.

Implementation

- Focus Groups: Organize focus groups with a diverse group of employees to discuss their experiences with chaplaincy services in a facilitated setting.

- Interviews: Conduct one-on-one interviews with employees who have used chaplaincy services to gather detailed feedback.

- Themes and Insights: Analyze the data collected to identify common themes and actionable insights.

Example Practice

Global Enterprises conducts quarterly focus groups and interviews with employees to gain a deeper understanding of their experiences with chaplaincy services. The insights gathered are used to refine and enhance the program.

3. Usage Metrics and Data Analysis

Definition and Importance

Tracking usage metrics and analyzing data helps to understand how chaplaincy services are being utilized and their impact on the organization.

Implementation

- Service Utilization: Monitor metrics such as the number of counseling sessions, attendance at workshops, and participation in support groups.

- Outcome Measures: Track outcomes such as employee well-being, job satisfaction, and retention rates.

- Data Analysis: Analyze the data to identify patterns and correlations between chaplaincy services and key organizational outcomes.

Example Practice

Wellness Tech Ltd. tracks usage metrics and key outcomes related to chaplaincy services. Data analysis reveals positive correlations between chaplaincy engagement and employee well-being, informing program adjustments.

4. Employee Well-Being Assessments

Definition and Importance

Assessing employee well-being provides insights into the overall impact of chaplaincy services on employees' mental, emotional, and spiritual health.

Implementation

- Well-Being Surveys: Administer surveys that measure various aspects of employee well-being, such as stress levels, emotional health, and job satisfaction.

- Regular Assessments: Conduct regular assessments to monitor changes in employee well-being over time.

- Comparative Analysis: Compare well-being data from employees who use chaplaincy services with those who do not to evaluate impact.

Example Practice

Creative Minds Corp regularly assesses employee well-being through surveys and compares the data between users and non-users of chaplaincy services, demonstrating the positive impact of the program.

5. Feedback from Managers and HR

Definition and Importance

Feedback from managers and HR provides a broader perspective on the impact of chaplaincy services on workplace culture and organizational outcomes.

Implementation

- Manager Surveys: Collect feedback from managers about the observed impact of chaplaincy services on their teams.

- HR Collaboration: Collaborate with HR to gather data on metrics such as absenteeism, turnover, and employee engagement.

- Holistic View: Use feedback to gain a holistic view of the chaplaincy program's effectiveness and areas for improvement.

Example Practice

At Global Enterprises, the corporate chaplain collaborates with HR and managers to gather feedback on the impact of chaplaincy services, providing a comprehensive view of the program's effectiveness.

Challenges and Solutions in Evaluating Chaplaincy Services

1. Ensuring Confidentiality and Trust

Definition and Importance

Maintaining confidentiality and trust is crucial when collecting feedback and data on chaplaincy services.

Challenges

- Sensitive Information: Employees may be reluctant to share feedback if they fear their confidentiality will be compromised.

- Trust Issues: Lack of trust in the evaluation process can result in incomplete or inaccurate data.

Solutions

- Anonymity: Ensure that surveys and feedback mechanisms are anonymous to protect employee confidentiality.

- Clear Communication: Communicate the importance of confidentiality and how data will be used to improve services.

- Secure Data Handling: Implement secure data handling practices to protect sensitive information.

Example Practice

Creative Minds Corp ensures anonymity in surveys and clearly communicates confidentiality measures, fostering trust and encouraging honest feedback from employees.

2. Collecting Representative Data

Definition and Importance

Collecting representative data ensures that the evaluation reflects the experiences and needs of the entire workforce.

Challenges

- Low Response Rates: Low participation in surveys and feedback mechanisms can result in unrepresentative data.

- Bias: Responses may be biased if certain groups are overrepresented or underrepresented.

Solutions

- Incentives: Offer incentives for participation in surveys and feedback mechanisms to increase response rates.

- Targeted Outreach: Conduct targeted outreach to ensure diverse participation across different employee groups.

- Balanced Sampling: Use balanced sampling techniques to gather representative data.

Example Practice

Global Enterprises uses targeted outreach and incentives to increase participation in surveys, ensuring that the data collected is representative of the entire workforce.

Conclusion

Evaluating the effectiveness of chaplaincy services is essential for understanding their impact, demonstrating their value, and continuously improving service delivery. By utilizing methods such as surveys and questionnaires, focus groups and interviews, usage metrics and data analysis, employee well-being assessments, and feedback from managers and HR, organizations can gain comprehensive insights into the effectiveness of their chaplaincy programs. Addressing challenges such as ensuring confidentiality and trust and collecting representative data is crucial for obtaining accurate and actionable feedback.

As we continue to explore the role of corporate chaplaincy in this book, we will delve into further strategies and best practices for addressing the common issues faced by employees. By understanding and addressing these challenges, organizations can create environments where employees feel valued, supported, and inspired.

Gathering and Analyzing Feedback from Employees

Introduction

Gathering and analyzing feedback from employees is crucial for assessing the effectiveness of chaplaincy services. This process provides valuable insights into employees' experiences and perceptions, guiding continuous improvement and demonstrating the value of chaplaincy programs. This chapter outlines methods for collecting and analyzing employee feedback, ensuring that chaplaincy services meet the needs and expectations of the workforce.

The Importance of Employee Feedback

1. Enhancing Service Delivery

Definition and Importance

Employee feedback helps to identify strengths and areas for improvement in chaplaincy services, leading to enhanced service delivery.

Impact

- Responsive Services: Allows for the adaptation of services to better meet employee needs.

- Quality Improvement: Drives continuous improvement by highlighting areas for development.

- Employee Satisfaction: Increases employee satisfaction by showing that their input is valued and acted upon.

Example

At Global Enterprises, regular employee feedback has led to the refinement of chaplaincy services, ensuring they are more responsive to employee needs and preferences.

2. Demonstrating Value and Impact

Definition and Importance

Feedback provides concrete evidence of the value and impact of chaplaincy services, helping to justify their existence and funding.

Impact

- Accountability: Demonstrates the effectiveness and accountability of chaplaincy programs.

- Stakeholder Engagement: Engages stakeholders by showing the positive impact of chaplaincy services on employee well-being.

- Informed Decision-Making: Provides data to support decisions about program development and resource allocation.

Example

Wellness Tech Ltd. uses employee feedback to demonstrate the positive impact of chaplaincy services, securing ongoing support and funding from stakeholders.

Methods for Gathering Employee Feedback

1. Surveys and Questionnaires

Definition and Importance

Surveys and questionnaires are structured tools for collecting quantitative and qualitative feedback from a broad range of employees.

Implementation

- Design: Develop surveys with clear, concise questions that cover key aspects of chaplaincy services, such as accessibility, quality, and impact.

- Distribution: Distribute surveys through various channels, such as email, intranet, or during company meetings, ensuring broad reach.

- Analysis: Analyze survey responses using statistical methods to identify trends and actionable insights.

Example Practice

At Creative Minds Corp, the corporate chaplain distributes biannual surveys to gather feedback on chaplaincy services, analyzing the data to inform program improvements.

2. Focus Groups

Definition and Importance

Focus groups involve facilitated discussions with a small, diverse group of employees to gather in-depth insights into their experiences with chaplaincy services.

Implementation

- Recruitment: Recruit a representative sample of employees to participate in focus groups, ensuring diversity in perspectives.

- Facilitation: Facilitate discussions using open-ended questions to encourage detailed feedback and candid conversation.

- Themes and Insights: Identify common themes and insights from focus group discussions to inform service enhancements.

Example Practice

Global Enterprises conducts quarterly focus groups to explore employee experiences with chaplaincy services, using the insights gathered to refine and improve the program.

3. One-on-One Interviews

Definition and Importance

One-on-one interviews provide an opportunity for employees to share detailed feedback in a confidential setting, offering deeper insights into their experiences.

Implementation

- Selection: Select a diverse range of employees for interviews to capture varied experiences and perspectives.

- Interview Guide: Develop an interview guide with open-ended questions to facilitate comprehensive discussions.

- Confidentiality: Ensure confidentiality to encourage honest and open feedback from employees.

Example Practice

At Wellness Tech Ltd., the corporate chaplain conducts one-on-one interviews with employees who have used chaplaincy services, gathering detailed feedback to enhance service delivery.

4. Suggestion Boxes

Definition and Importance

Suggestion boxes provide a simple, anonymous way for employees to offer feedback and suggestions about chaplaincy services.

Implementation

- Placement: Place suggestion boxes in accessible locations throughout the workplace, such as break rooms and common areas.

- Regular Review: Review suggestions regularly to identify common themes and actionable feedback.

- Response and Action: Communicate how suggestions are being addressed and any resulting changes to chaplaincy services.

Example Practice

Creative Minds Corp uses suggestion boxes to collect anonymous feedback from employees, regularly reviewing and acting on the suggestions to improve chaplaincy services.

5. Online Feedback Platforms

Definition and Importance

Online feedback platforms allow employees to provide feedback at their convenience, making the process more accessible and efficient.

Implementation

- Platform Selection: Choose a user-friendly online platform for collecting and managing employee feedback.

- Promotion: Promote the platform through internal communications to ensure employees are aware of and use it.

- Data Analysis: Use analytics tools provided by the platform to analyze feedback and identify trends.

Example Practice

Global Enterprises implements an online feedback platform, encouraging employees to share their experiences with chaplaincy services at their convenience and using the data to guide improvements.

Analyzing Employee Feedback

1. Quantitative Analysis

Definition and Importance

Quantitative analysis involves analyzing numerical data from surveys and feedback platforms to identify patterns and trends.

Implementation

- Statistical Tools: Use statistical tools and software to analyze quantitative data, such as response frequencies, averages, and trends over time.

- Key Metrics: Identify key metrics, such as satisfaction scores and service usage rates, to measure the effectiveness of chaplaincy services.

- Benchmarking: Compare metrics against benchmarks or previous data to assess performance and improvement.

Example Practice

At Creative Minds Corp, the corporate chaplain uses statistical software to analyze survey data, identifying key metrics and trends to inform service enhancements.

2. Qualitative Analysis

Definition and Importance

Qualitative analysis involves analyzing textual data from focus groups, interviews, and open-ended survey responses to gain deeper insights into employee experiences.

Implementation

- Thematic Analysis: Conduct thematic analysis to identify common themes and patterns in qualitative data.

- Coding and Categorization: Use coding and categorization to organize qualitative data and facilitate analysis.

- Narrative Insights: Extract narrative insights that provide context and depth to quantitative findings.

Example Practice

Global Enterprises conducts thematic analysis of focus group and interview data, identifying common themes and insights to guide chaplaincy service improvements.

3. Integrating Quantitative and Qualitative Data

Definition and Importance

Integrating quantitative and qualitative data provides a comprehensive understanding of the impact and effectiveness of chaplaincy services.

Implementation

- Mixed Methods: Use mixed methods to combine quantitative and qualitative data, providing a fuller picture of employee experiences.

- Cross-Validation: Cross-validate findings from different data sources to ensure accuracy and reliability.

- Holistic Insights: Develop holistic insights that incorporate both numerical trends and narrative context.

Example Practice

At Wellness Tech Ltd., the corporate chaplain integrates quantitative survey data with qualitative insights from interviews, providing a comprehensive evaluation of chaplaincy services.

Challenges and Solutions in Gathering and Analyzing Feedback

1. Ensuring High Response Rates

Definition and Importance

High response rates are essential for collecting representative data that accurately reflects employee experiences and needs.

Challenges

- Low Participation: Employees may be reluctant to participate in feedback mechanisms due to time constraints or lack of awareness.

- Bias: Low participation can result in biased data if certain groups are underrepresented.

Solutions

- Incentives: Offer incentives, such as gift cards or recognition, to encourage participation in surveys and feedback mechanisms.

- Communication Campaigns: Conduct communication campaigns to raise awareness about the importance of feedback and how it will be used.

- Convenient Options: Provide multiple, convenient options for providing feedback, such as online platforms and mobile apps.

Example Practice

Creative Minds Corp uses incentives and communication campaigns to increase participation in feedback mechanisms, ensuring high response rates and representative data.

2. Maintaining Confidentiality and Trust

Definition and Importance

Maintaining confidentiality and trust is crucial for encouraging honest and open feedback from employees.

Challenges

- Fear of Reprisal: Employees may fear reprisal or negative consequences for providing candid feedback.

- Confidentiality Concerns: Concerns about confidentiality can deter employees from sharing their true experiences.

Solutions

- Anonymous Feedback: Ensure that feedback mechanisms allow for anonymous responses to protect employee confidentiality.

- Clear Policies: Communicate clear policies about how feedback will be used and the measures in place to protect confidentiality.

- Trust Building: Build trust by consistently acting on feedback and demonstrating that employee input is valued and respected.

Example Practice

Global Enterprises ensures that all feedback mechanisms are anonymous and communicates clear policies to protect confidentiality, fostering trust and encouraging honest feedback.

Conclusion

Gathering and analyzing feedback from employees is essential for evaluating the effectiveness of chaplaincy services and driving continuous improvement. By using methods such as surveys and questionnaires, focus groups, one-on-one interviews, suggestion boxes, and online feedback platforms, organizations can collect comprehensive feedback from employees. Analyzing this feedback through quantitative and qualitative methods provides valuable insights into the impact of chaplaincy services, guiding enhancements and demonstrating their value. Addressing challenges such as ensuring high response rates and maintaining confidentiality and trust is crucial for obtaining accurate and actionable feedback.

As we continue to explore the role of corporate chaplaincy in this book, we will delve into further strategies and best practices for addressing the common issues faced by employees. By understanding and addressing these challenges, organizations can create environments where employees feel valued, supported, and inspired.

Reporting and Communicating Results to Management

Introduction

Effectively reporting and communicating the results of chaplaincy service evaluations to management is essential for demonstrating the value and impact of these programs. Clear and compelling communication helps secure support, funding, and commitment from organizational leaders. This chapter outlines strategies for reporting and communicating the results of chaplaincy service evaluations to management, ensuring that the insights gained are understood and acted upon.

The Importance of Effective Reporting and Communication

1. Demonstrating Value and Impact

Definition and Importance

Reporting the results of chaplaincy service evaluations demonstrates the tangible benefits and impact of these programs on employee well-being and organizational outcomes.

Impact

- Justification of Programs: Provides evidence to justify the continuation and expansion of chaplaincy services.

- Stakeholder Engagement: Engages stakeholders by showing the positive impact of chaplaincy services.

- Resource Allocation: Supports informed decision-making about resource allocation and program development.

Example

At Global Enterprises, detailed reports on chaplaincy service evaluations have helped secure ongoing support and funding from management by clearly demonstrating the program's positive impact on employee well-being.

2. Guiding Strategic Decisions

Definition and Importance

Communicating evaluation results effectively helps guide strategic decisions about the development and implementation of chaplaincy services.

Impact

- Program Development: Informs the development of new initiatives and the refinement of existing services.

- Policy Formulation: Supports the formulation of policies that enhance employee well-being and workplace culture.

- Strategic Planning: Aligns chaplaincy services with broader organizational goals and strategies.

Example

Wellness Tech Ltd. uses evaluation reports to guide strategic decisions about chaplaincy services, ensuring they align with the company's mission and goals.

Methods for Reporting Evaluation Results

1. Written Reports

Definition and Importance

Written reports provide a detailed and structured presentation of evaluation results, offering comprehensive insights into the effectiveness of chaplaincy services.

Implementation

- Executive Summary: Begin with an executive summary that highlights key findings, conclusions, and recommendations.

- Detailed Analysis: Include detailed analysis sections that present quantitative and qualitative data, key metrics, and thematic insights.

- Visual Aids: Use visual aids, such as charts, graphs, and tables, to illustrate key points and make the data more accessible.

- Recommendations: Conclude with actionable recommendations based on the evaluation findings.

Example Practice

At Creative Minds Corp, the corporate chaplain prepares written reports with executive summaries, detailed analyses, visual aids, and recommendations, providing management with clear and comprehensive insights.

2. Presentations

Definition and Importance

Presentations offer a dynamic way to communicate evaluation results to management, facilitating engagement and discussion.

Implementation

- Structured Format: Structure the presentation to cover key findings, analysis, and recommendations in a clear and logical sequence.

- Engaging Visuals: Use engaging visuals, such as slides, infographics, and video clips, to enhance understanding and retention.

- Interactive Elements: Incorporate interactive elements, such as Q&A sessions and discussion points, to encourage engagement and feedback.

- Tailored Content: Tailor the content to the audience, focusing on aspects most relevant to management's interests and concerns.

Example Practice

Global Enterprises' corporate chaplain delivers engaging presentations to management, using visuals and interactive elements to effectively communicate evaluation results and encourage discussion.

3. Dashboards and Scorecards

Definition and Importance

Dashboards and scorecards provide a concise and visual summary of key performance indicators (KPIs) and metrics related to chaplaincy services.

Implementation

- Key Metrics: Identify and include key metrics that reflect the effectiveness and impact of chaplaincy services, such as usage rates, satisfaction scores, and well-being measures.

- Visual Design: Design dashboards and scorecards with clear, easy-to-understand visuals, such as bar charts, pie charts, and trend lines.

- Real-Time Data: Use tools that allow for real-time data updates, providing management with current and relevant information.

- Accessibility: Ensure that dashboards and scorecards are easily accessible to management, such as through online platforms or regular email updates.

Example Practice

Wellness Tech Ltd. uses online dashboards to provide management with real-time updates on key metrics related to chaplaincy services, ensuring that leaders have access to current and actionable data.

4. Executive Summaries

Definition and Importance

Executive summaries provide a concise overview of evaluation results, highlighting key findings and recommendations without delving into detailed analysis.

Implementation

- Concise Content: Summarize key findings and recommendations in a concise and straightforward manner, typically one to two pages.

- Focus on Impact: Highlight the most significant impacts of chaplaincy services on employee well-being and organizational outcomes.

- Actionable Recommendations: Include clear and actionable recommendations for management to consider.

- Visual Elements: Use visual elements, such as bullet points and charts, to enhance clarity and readability.

Example Practice

At Creative Minds Corp, the corporate chaplain provides executive summaries to management, summarizing key findings and recommendations in a clear and concise format.

Strategies for Effective Communication

1. Tailoring the Message

Definition and Importance

Tailoring the message involves customizing the content and delivery of evaluation results to meet the specific needs and interests of the management audience.

Implementation

- Understand the Audience: Consider the interests, priorities, and concerns of the management audience when preparing the report or presentation.

- Relevant Content: Focus on the aspects of the evaluation that are most relevant to the audience, such as cost-effectiveness, employee engagement, or alignment with organizational goals.

- Customized Recommendations: Provide recommendations that are tailored to the specific context and strategic objectives of the organization.

Example Practice

Global Enterprises' corporate chaplain tailors evaluation reports to address the specific interests of different management teams, ensuring that the message resonates and is impactful.

2. Using Clear and Compelling Language

Definition and Importance

Using clear and compelling language helps ensure that evaluation results are easily understood and persuasive to management.

Implementation

- Avoid Jargon: Avoid technical jargon and use plain language to ensure clarity and accessibility.

- Highlight Key Points: Emphasize key findings and recommendations, using bullet points and headings to guide the reader's attention.

- Compelling Narratives: Use compelling narratives and real-life examples to illustrate the impact of chaplaincy services and make the data more relatable.

Example Practice

At Creative Minds Corp, the corporate chaplain uses clear and compelling language in reports and presentations, making the evaluation results accessible and persuasive to management.

3. Engaging Stakeholders

Definition and Importance

Engaging stakeholders in the communication process ensures that they understand and support the findings and recommendations of the evaluation.

Implementation

- Interactive Presentations: Use interactive presentations that encourage questions, discussions, and feedback from management.

- Stakeholder Meetings: Organize meetings with key stakeholders to discuss evaluation results and gather input on recommendations.

- Collaborative Approach: Foster a collaborative approach by involving stakeholders in the development of action plans based on evaluation findings.

Example Practice

Wellness Tech Ltd. engages stakeholders through interactive presentations and meetings, ensuring that management understands and supports the evaluation findings and recommendations.

4. Continuous Follow-Up

Definition and Importance

Continuous follow-up ensures that the insights and recommendations from the evaluation are acted upon and that progress is monitored.

Implementation

- Regular Updates: Provide regular updates to management on the implementation of recommendations and the progress of chaplaincy services.

- Progress Reports: Share progress reports that highlight key achievements, challenges, and adjustments based on ongoing feedback and data.

- Feedback Loop: Establish a feedback loop where management can provide input and suggestions for further improvements.

Example Practice

At Creative Minds Corp, the corporate chaplain provides regular progress reports to management, ensuring continuous follow-up and engagement with the evaluation process.

Challenges and Solutions in Reporting and Communicating Results

1. Managing Data Overload

Definition and Importance

Managing data overload involves presenting evaluation results in a clear and concise manner to avoid overwhelming management with too much information.

Challenges

- Complex Data: The evaluation process can generate large amounts of complex data.

- Attention Span: Management may have limited time and attention for reviewing detailed reports.

Solutions

- Prioritize Key Findings: Focus on the most important and impactful findings and recommendations.

- Use Summaries and Visuals: Use executive summaries, bullet points, and visual aids to present key information concisely.

- Highlight Actionable Insights: Emphasize actionable insights and recommendations to guide decision-making.

Example Practice

Global Enterprises' corporate chaplain prioritizes key findings and uses executive summaries and visuals to present evaluation results concisely and effectively.

2. Ensuring Data Accuracy and Credibility

Definition and Importance

Ensuring data accuracy and credibility is crucial for building trust and confidence in the evaluation results.

Challenges

- Data Quality: Ensuring that the data collected is accurate, reliable, and valid.

- Credibility: Demonstrating the credibility of the evaluation process and findings to management.

Solutions

- Rigorous Data Collection: Use rigorous data collection methods and tools to ensure data quality.

- Transparent Methodology: Provide a transparent explanation of the evaluation methodology and data analysis process.

- Third-Party Validation: Consider using third-party validation or external audits to enhance credibility.

Example Practice

At Creative Minds Corp, the corporate chaplain uses rigorous data collection methods and provides a transparent methodology in reports, ensuring data accuracy and credibility.

Conclusion

Effectively reporting and communicating the results of chaplaincy service evaluations to management is essential for demonstrating

their value and impact, guiding strategic decisions, and securing support. By using methods such as written reports, presentations, dashboards, and executive summaries, and by employing strategies such as tailoring the message, using clear and compelling language, engaging stakeholders, and ensuring continuous follow-up, organizations can ensure that the insights gained from evaluations are understood and acted upon. Addressing challenges such as managing data overload and ensuring data accuracy and credibility is crucial for effective communication and engagement.

As we continue to explore the role of corporate chaplaincy in this book, we will delve into further strategies and best practices for addressing the common issues faced by

employees. By understanding and addressing these challenges, organizations can create environments where employees feel valued, supported, and inspired.

Demonstrating Value

Linking Spiritual Well-Being to Productivity and Morale

Introduction

Demonstrating the value of chaplaincy services involves clearly linking spiritual well-being to key organizational outcomes such as productivity and morale. By highlighting these connections, chaplains can show how their work contributes to the overall success and well-being of the organization. This chapter explores strategies for demonstrating the value of chaplaincy services by linking spiritual well-being to productivity and morale.

The Importance of Demonstrating Value

1. Securing Support and Funding

Definition and Importance

Demonstrating the value of chaplaincy services helps secure ongoing support and funding from organizational leaders by showing the tangible benefits of these programs.

Impact

- Resource Allocation: Justifies the allocation of resources to chaplaincy services.

- Stakeholder Engagement: Engages stakeholders by highlighting the positive impact of chaplaincy services on organizational outcomes.

- Sustainability: Ensures the sustainability and growth of chaplaincy programs by demonstrating their value.

Example

At Global Enterprises, demonstrating the value of chaplaincy services has helped secure consistent funding and support from management, ensuring the program's sustainability.

2. Enhancing Organizational Well-Being

Definition and Importance

Linking spiritual well-being to productivity and morale enhances overall organizational well-being by showing how chaplaincy services contribute to a positive work environment.

Impact

- Improved Morale: Demonstrates how chaplaincy services improve employee morale and job satisfaction.

- Increased Productivity: Shows the connection between spiritual well-being and enhanced productivity.

- Positive Culture: Contributes to a positive and supportive workplace culture.

Example

Wellness Tech Ltd. has seen improvements in employee morale and productivity as a direct result of chaplaincy services, contributing to a more positive and productive work environment.

Strategies for Demonstrating Value

1. Collecting and Analyzing Data

Definition and Importance

Collecting and analyzing data on the impact of chaplaincy services is essential for demonstrating their value and linking spiritual well-being to productivity and morale.

Implementation

- Key Metrics: Identify key metrics related to spiritual well-being, productivity, and morale, such as employee engagement scores, absenteeism rates, and productivity measures.

- Data Collection: Collect data through surveys, usage metrics, and employee feedback to assess the impact of chaplaincy services.

- Data Analysis: Analyze the data to identify correlations and trends that link spiritual well-being to productivity and morale.

Example Practice

At Creative Minds Corp, the corporate chaplain collects and analyzes data on employee engagement, absenteeism, and productivity to demonstrate the impact of chaplaincy services on these key metrics.

2. Using Case Studies and Testimonials

Definition and Importance

Case studies and testimonials provide qualitative evidence of the value of chaplaincy services, highlighting personal experiences and successes.

Implementation

- Case Studies: Develop case studies that showcase specific examples of how chaplaincy services have positively impacted individual employees and teams.

- Testimonials: Gather testimonials from employees who have benefited from chaplaincy services, highlighting their experiences and outcomes.

- Storytelling: Use storytelling to present case studies and testimonials in a compelling and relatable way.

Example Practice

Global Enterprises uses case studies and testimonials to illustrate the positive impact of chaplaincy services on employees' well-being, productivity, and morale, making a compelling case for their value.

3. Linking to Organizational Outcomes

Definition and Importance

Clearly linking chaplaincy services to organizational outcomes such as productivity, retention, and employee satisfaction demonstrates their value in contributing to the organization's success.

Implementation

- Outcome Measures: Identify and measure key organizational outcomes that can be influenced by chaplaincy services, such as retention rates, employee satisfaction, and performance metrics.

- Correlation Analysis: Conduct correlation analysis to link chaplaincy services to improvements in these outcomes.

- Visual Representation: Use charts, graphs, and other visual aids to clearly present the link between chaplaincy services and organizational outcomes.

Example Practice

Wellness Tech Ltd. presents data showing the correlation between chaplaincy service usage and improved retention rates, employee satisfaction scores, and productivity metrics, demonstrating the value of these services.

4. Engaging with Management and Stakeholders

Definition and Importance

Engaging with management and stakeholders involves presenting the value of chaplaincy services in a way that resonates with their interests and concerns.

Implementation

- Targeted Presentations: Develop presentations that focus on the aspects of chaplaincy services most relevant to management and stakeholders, such as cost savings, employee retention, and productivity improvements.

- Regular Updates: Provide regular updates on the impact of chaplaincy services, highlighting key successes and areas for improvement.

- Collaborative Approach: Engage stakeholders in discussions about chaplaincy services, seeking their input and collaboration in enhancing the program.

Example Practice

At Creative Minds Corp, the corporate chaplain regularly presents updates to management on the impact of chaplaincy services, engaging them in discussions about the program's successes and future direction.

Linking Spiritual Well-Being to Productivity and Morale

1. Improving Employee Engagement

Definition and Importance

Spiritual well-being contributes to higher employee engagement, leading to increased productivity and job satisfaction.

Implementation

- Engagement Surveys: Conduct regular employee engagement surveys to assess the impact of chaplaincy services on engagement levels.

- Focus Groups: Organize focus groups to explore how chaplaincy services influence employee engagement and job satisfaction.

- Engagement Initiatives: Develop initiatives that link chaplaincy services to broader employee engagement efforts, such as wellness programs and team-building activities.

Example Practice

Global Enterprises uses engagement surveys and focus groups to demonstrate how chaplaincy services enhance employee engagement, linking these improvements to increased productivity and morale.

2. Reducing Absenteeism and Turnover

Definition and Importance

Spiritual well-being can reduce absenteeism and turnover by addressing underlying issues that contribute to employee stress and dissatisfaction.

Implementation

- Absenteeism Data: Track absenteeism rates and analyze the impact of chaplaincy services on reducing absenteeism.

- Turnover Rates: Monitor turnover rates and assess how chaplaincy services influence employee retention.

- Support Programs: Develop support programs that address common causes of absenteeism and turnover, such as stress management and conflict resolution.

Example Practice

Wellness Tech Ltd. tracks absenteeism and turnover rates, demonstrating how chaplaincy services contribute to reducing these metrics and improving overall productivity.

3. Enhancing Job Satisfaction

Definition and Importance

Spiritual well-being contributes to higher job satisfaction by providing employees with the support and resources they need to thrive.

Implementation

- Satisfaction Surveys: Conduct job satisfaction surveys to measure the impact of chaplaincy services on employee satisfaction levels.

- One-on-One Interviews: Conduct one-on-one interviews with employees to gather detailed feedback on how chaplaincy services enhance their job satisfaction.

- Program Integration: Integrate chaplaincy services with other initiatives aimed at improving job satisfaction, such as professional development and recognition programs.

Example Practice

At Creative Minds Corp, job satisfaction surveys and interviews reveal that employees who use chaplaincy services report higher levels of satisfaction, demonstrating the value of these services in enhancing morale.

4. Supporting Mental Health and Well-Being

Definition and Importance

Spiritual well-being supports overall mental health and well-being, leading to better performance and reduced stress levels.

Implementation

- Well-Being Assessments: Conduct regular assessments of employee mental health and well-being to measure the impact of chaplaincy services.

- Counseling Services: Offer counseling and support services that address mental health issues, reducing stress and improving productivity.

- Wellness Programs: Integrate chaplaincy services with broader wellness programs to provide comprehensive support for employee well-being.

Example Practice

Global Enterprises conducts well-being assessments and integrates chaplaincy services with wellness programs, demonstrating how these services support mental health and enhance productivity and morale.

Challenges and Solutions in Demonstrating Value

1. Quantifying Intangible Benefits

Definition and Importance

Quantifying the intangible benefits of chaplaincy services, such as spiritual well-being and emotional support, can be challenging but is essential for demonstrating value.

Challenges

- Subjectivity: Intangible benefits are often subjective and difficult to measure.

- Data Collection: Collecting data on intangible benefits requires thoughtful and sensitive approaches.

Solutions

- Mixed Methods: Use a combination of quantitative and qualitative methods to capture both measurable outcomes and personal experiences.

- Proxy Measures: Identify proxy measures that can serve as indicators of intangible benefits, such as employee engagement and satisfaction scores.

- Narrative Evidence: Complement quantitative data with narrative evidence, such as case studies and testimonials.

Example Practice

At Creative Minds Corp, the corporate chaplain uses mixed methods and proxy measures to capture the intangible benefits of chaplaincy services, providing a comprehensive view of their value.

2. Ensuring Consistent Measurement

Definition and Importance

Consistent measurement of the impact of chaplaincy services ensures that data is reliable and comparable over time.

Challenges

- Measurement Variability: Inconsistent measurement methods can lead to unreliable data.

- Longitudinal Data: Collecting and analyzing longitudinal data requires sustained effort and resources.

Solutions

- Standardized Tools: Use standardized measurement tools and methods to ensure consistency.

- Regular Assessments: Conduct regular assessments to track changes and trends over time.

- Long-Term Commitment: Commit to long-term data collection and analysis to build a comprehensive understanding of impact.

Example Practice

Global Enterprises uses standardized tools and conducts regular assessments to ensure

consistent measurement of the impact of chaplaincy services, building a reliable data set over time.

Conclusion

Demonstrating the value of chaplaincy services involves clearly linking spiritual well-being to key organizational outcomes such as productivity and morale. By collecting and analyzing data, using case studies and testimonials, linking to organizational outcomes, and engaging with management and stakeholders, chaplains can effectively demonstrate the impact of their work. Addressing challenges such as quantifying intangible benefits and ensuring consistent measurement is crucial for providing a comprehensive and compelling case for the value of chaplaincy services.

As we continue to explore the role of corporate chaplaincy in this book, we will delve into further strategies and best practices for addressing the common issues faced by employees. By understanding and addressing these challenges, organizations can create environments where employees feel valued, supported, and inspired.

Case Studies and Success Stories

Introduction

Case studies and success stories are powerful tools for demonstrating the impact of chaplaincy services. They provide real-life examples of how these services have positively affected individuals and the organization, highlighting the tangible benefits and successes. This chapter explores the importance of case studies and success stories, offering guidance on how to effectively gather and present these narratives to showcase the value of chaplaincy programs.

The Importance of Case Studies and Success Stories

1. Illustrating Impact

Definition and Importance

Case studies and success stories provide concrete examples of how chaplaincy services have made a difference, illustrating the impact of these programs on individual and organizational well-being.

Impact

- Real-Life Examples: Offer real-life examples that demonstrate the positive effects of chaplaincy services.

- Humanizing Data: Add a human element to quantitative data, making the impact more relatable and compelling.

- Emotional Connection: Create an emotional connection with the audience, fostering greater understanding and support.

Example

At Global Enterprises, case studies highlighting personal stories of employees who have benefited from chaplaincy services have been instrumental in illustrating the program's positive impact.

2. Building Credibility and Trust

Definition and Importance

Sharing success stories builds credibility and trust in chaplaincy services by showing real outcomes and testimonials from those who have experienced the benefits firsthand.

Impact

- Authenticity: Provides authentic testimonials that enhance the credibility of chaplaincy services.

- Trust Building: Builds trust with employees and stakeholders by demonstrating transparency and effectiveness.

- Reputation Enhancement: Enhances the organization's reputation as a supportive and caring employer.

Example

Wellness Tech Ltd. has built credibility and trust in its chaplaincy services by sharing success stories from employees who have experienced significant improvements in their well-being and job satisfaction.

Gathering Case Studies and Success Stories

1. Identifying Suitable Candidates

Definition and Importance

Identifying employees who have had positive experiences with chaplaincy services is the first step in gathering compelling case studies and success stories.

Implementation

- Employee Feedback: Use feedback from surveys, interviews, and focus groups to identify employees who have benefited from chaplaincy services.

- Chaplain Referrals: Ask chaplains to refer employees who have experienced positive outcomes.

- Voluntary Participation: Ensure that participation is voluntary and that employees are willing to share their stories.

Example Practice

At Creative Minds Corp, the corporate chaplain identifies suitable candidates for case studies by reviewing feedback and seeking referrals from chaplains, ensuring that participation is voluntary and enthusiastic.

2. Conducting Interviews

Definition and Importance

Conducting interviews with employees who have benefited from chaplaincy services provides detailed insights and personal narratives that form the basis of compelling case studies.

Implementation

- Interview Preparation: Prepare a list of open-ended questions to guide the interview and elicit detailed responses.

- Confidentiality Assurance: Assure participants of confidentiality and obtain their consent to share their stories.

- Recording and Transcription: Record the interviews (with permission) and transcribe them for accuracy and completeness.

Example Practice

Global Enterprises conducts interviews with employees who have benefited from chaplaincy services, using open-ended questions to gather detailed narratives and ensure confidentiality and consent.

3. Developing the Narrative

Definition and Importance

Developing the narrative involves crafting the raw interview data into a cohesive and compelling story that highlights the impact of chaplaincy services.

Implementation

- Story Structure: Structure the story with a clear beginning, middle, and end, highlighting the employee's initial situation, the intervention of chaplaincy services, and the positive outcomes.

- Key Themes: Identify and emphasize key themes that illustrate the benefits of chaplaincy services, such as improved well-being, increased job satisfaction, and personal growth.

- Quotes and Anecdotes: Include direct quotes and anecdotes from the interviews to add authenticity and emotional impact.

Example Practice

Wellness Tech Ltd. develops compelling narratives from interview data, structuring the stories to highlight key themes and including quotes and anecdotes to enhance authenticity and emotional impact.

4. Using Visual and Multimedia Elements

Definition and Importance

Incorporating visual and multimedia elements can enhance the storytelling process, making case studies and success stories more engaging and impactful.

Implementation

- Photographs and Videos: Use photographs and videos of the employees (with consent) to add a visual element to the stories.

- Infographics: Create infographics that summarize key points and highlight the impact of chaplaincy services.

- Digital Formats: Present the stories in digital formats, such as online articles, video testimonials, and social media posts, to reach a broader audience.

Example Practice

At Creative Minds Corp, case studies and success stories are presented with photographs, videos, and infographics, making them more engaging and accessible to a wide audience.

Presenting Case Studies and Success Stories

1. Written Reports and Publications

Definition and Importance

Written reports and publications provide a formal and detailed presentation of case studies and success stories, suitable for sharing with management and stakeholders.

Implementation

- Report Structure: Include case studies and success stories as a section in written evaluation reports or as standalone publications.

- Detailed Narratives: Present detailed narratives that highlight individual experiences and outcomes.

- Supporting Data: Complement the stories with supporting data and analysis to provide a comprehensive view of the impact.

Example Practice

Global Enterprises includes case studies and success stories in its annual evaluation reports, providing detailed narratives supported by data to illustrate the impact of chaplaincy services.

2. Presentations and Meetings

Definition and Importance

Presenting case studies and success stories in meetings and presentations provides an opportunity to engage directly with management and stakeholders, facilitating discussion and feedback.

Implementation

- Presentation Slides: Use presentation slides to highlight key points from the stories, supported by visual and multimedia elements.

- Interactive Discussion: Encourage interactive discussion by inviting questions and feedback from the audience.

- Highlighting Impact: Emphasize the impact of chaplaincy services on individual employees and the organization as a whole.

Example Practice

Wellness Tech Ltd. presents case studies and success stories in quarterly management meetings, using slides and videos to engage the audience and highlight the impact of chaplaincy services.

3. Internal Communications

Definition and Importance

Sharing case studies and success stories through internal communications channels helps raise awareness and support for chaplaincy services among employees.

Implementation

- Newsletters: Include case studies and success stories in internal newsletters to keep employees informed and engaged.

- Intranet: Publish stories on the company intranet, making them easily accessible to all employees.

- Emails and Bulletins: Share stories through regular email updates and bulletins to reach a wide audience.

Example Practice

At Creative Minds Corp, case studies and success stories are featured in internal newsletters and published on the company intranet, ensuring that employees are aware of the positive impact of chaplaincy services.

4. External Communications

Definition and Importance

Sharing case studies and success stories through external communications channels enhances the organization's reputation and showcases its commitment to employee well-being.

Implementation

- Website: Publish case studies and success stories on the company website to reach external audiences, such as clients, partners, and potential employees.

- Social Media: Share stories on social media platforms to engage with a broader audience and highlight the organization's values.

- Press Releases: Use press releases to share significant success stories with the media, enhancing public awareness and reputation.

Example Practice

Global Enterprises publishes case studies and success stories on its website and shares them on social media, highlighting its commitment to employee well-being and enhancing its public image.

Challenges and Solutions in Sharing Case Studies and Success Stories

1. Ensuring Authenticity and Consent

Definition and Importance

Ensuring the authenticity of the stories and obtaining consent from participants is crucial for maintaining credibility and ethical standards.

Challenges

- Authenticity: Ensuring that the stories are genuine and accurately reflect the participants' experiences.

- Consent: Obtaining informed consent from participants to share their stories publicly.

Solutions

- Accurate Representation: Ensure that the stories accurately represent the participants' experiences and outcomes.

- Informed Consent: Obtain informed consent from participants, clearly explaining how their stories will be used and shared.

- Confidentiality: Respect participants' wishes regarding anonymity and confidentiality.

Example Practice

At Creative Minds Corp, the corporate chaplain ensures that case studies and success stories accurately represent participants' experiences and obtain informed consent before sharing them.

2. Balancing Privacy and Impact

Definition and Importance

Balancing the need to protect participants' privacy with the desire to maximize the impact of the stories is essential for ethical storytelling.

Challenges

- Privacy Concerns: Participants may have concerns about their privacy and the public sharing of their stories.

- Impact: Detailed and personal stories often have a greater impact but may raise privacy issues.

Solutions

- Anonymity Options: Offer participants the option to share their stories anonymously or with pseudonyms.

- Selective Details: Share only the necessary details that illustrate the impact, protecting sensitive information.

- Participant Control: Give participants control over which aspects of their stories are shared and how they are presented.

Example Practice

Global Enterprises respects participants' privacy by offering anonymity options and sharing only necessary details, ensuring that the stories have an impact while protecting sensitive information.

Conclusion

Case studies and success stories are powerful tools for demonstrating the impact of chaplaincy services, illustrating their value through real-life examples and personal narratives. By gathering detailed stories, using visual and multimedia elements, and presenting them through various channels, chaplains can effectively showcase the benefits of their programs. Addressing challenges such as ensuring authenticity, obtaining consent, and balancing privacy with impact is crucial for ethical and effective storytelling.

As we continue to explore the role of corporate chaplaincy in this book, we will delve into further strategies and best practices for addressing the common issues faced by employees. By understanding and addressing these challenges, organizations can create environments where employees feel valued, supported, and inspired.

Building the Case for Ongoing Support and Investment

Introduction

Securing ongoing support and investment for chaplaincy services requires a compelling case that demonstrates their value and impact on the organization. This involves presenting evidence, success stories, and strategic recommendations that resonate with stakeholders and decision-makers. This chapter explores strategies for building a robust case for continued support and investment in chaplaincy programs.

The Importance of Ongoing Support and Investment

1. Sustaining Program Effectiveness

Definition and Importance

Ongoing support and investment ensure the sustainability and effectiveness of chaplaincy services, allowing them to continue meeting the needs of employees.

Impact

- Resource Availability: Ensures that sufficient resources are available to maintain and enhance chaplaincy services.

- Program Expansion: Enables the expansion of services to reach more employees and address emerging needs.

- Continuous Improvement: Supports continuous improvement initiatives that enhance the quality and impact of chaplaincy programs.

Example

At Global Enterprises, ongoing support and investment have enabled the chaplaincy program to expand its services and implement continuous improvement initiatives, resulting in enhanced employee well-being.

2. Demonstrating Organizational Commitment

Definition and Importance

Investing in chaplaincy services demonstrates the organization's commitment to employee well-being, fostering a positive and supportive workplace culture.

Impact

- Employee Morale: Boosts employee morale by showing that the organization values and supports their well-being.

- Attracting Talent: Attracts and retains top talent by highlighting the organization's commitment to creating a supportive work environment.

- Positive Reputation: Enhances the organization's reputation as an employer of choice that prioritizes employee well-being.

Example

Wellness Tech Ltd. has attracted and retained top talent by demonstrating its commitment to employee well-being through ongoing investment in chaplaincy services.

Strategies for Building the Case for Ongoing Support and Investment

1. Presenting Comprehensive Data and Evidence

Definition and Importance

Presenting comprehensive data and evidence is essential for demonstrating the impact and value of chaplaincy services to stakeholders and decision-makers.

Implementation

- Quantitative Data: Present quantitative data on key metrics such as employee engagement, absenteeism, turnover, and productivity to show the impact of chaplaincy services.

- Qualitative Data: Include qualitative data from surveys, interviews, and focus groups to provide a deeper understanding of the personal and emotional impact of chaplaincy services.

- Case Studies and Success Stories: Use case studies and success stories to illustrate the real-life benefits of chaplaincy services.

Example Practice

At Creative Minds Corp, the corporate chaplain presents comprehensive data and evidence, including quantitative metrics and qualitative insights, to demonstrate the value of chaplaincy services to management.

2. Highlighting Return on Investment (ROI)

Definition and Importance

Highlighting the return on investment (ROI) of chaplaincy services shows how these programs contribute to the organization's financial and operational success.

Implementation

- Cost-Benefit Analysis: Conduct a cost-benefit analysis to compare the costs of chaplaincy services with the financial benefits, such as reduced absenteeism and turnover costs.

- Productivity Gains: Highlight productivity gains resulting from improved employee well-being and engagement.

- Healthcare Savings: Present data on healthcare savings resulting from reduced stress and improved mental health among employees.

Example Practice

Global Enterprises conducts a cost-benefit analysis to demonstrate the ROI of chaplaincy services, showing how the financial benefits outweigh the costs and contribute to the organization's success.

3. Aligning with Organizational Goals and Values

Definition and Importance

Aligning chaplaincy services with the organization's goals and values helps demonstrate their strategic relevance and importance.

Implementation

- Mission Alignment: Show how chaplaincy services align with the organization's mission and core values, such as promoting employee well-being and creating a supportive workplace culture.

- Strategic Objectives: Link chaplaincy services to the organization's strategic objectives, such as enhancing employee engagement and reducing turnover.

- Cultural Fit: Highlight how chaplaincy services contribute to building a positive and inclusive workplace culture.

Example Practice

Wellness Tech Ltd. aligns its chaplaincy services with the organization's mission and strategic objectives, demonstrating their relevance and importance to the overall organizational goals.

4. Engaging Key Stakeholders

Definition and Importance

Engaging key stakeholders in the process of building the case for ongoing support and investment ensures their buy-in and support.

Implementation

- Stakeholder Involvement: Involve key stakeholders, such as senior management, HR, and employee representatives, in discussions about the impact and future direction of chaplaincy services.

- Feedback and Input: Gather feedback and input from stakeholders to understand their perspectives and address any concerns or suggestions.

- Collaborative Approach: Foster a collaborative approach by working with stakeholders to develop and implement strategies for enhancing chaplaincy services.

Example Practice

At Creative Minds Corp, the corporate chaplain engages key stakeholders through regular meetings and discussions, ensuring their buy-in and support for ongoing investment in chaplaincy services.

5. Communicating Successes and Impact

Definition and Importance

Regularly communicating the successes and impact of chaplaincy services helps maintain visibility and support for these programs.

Implementation

- Regular Updates: Provide regular updates on the impact of chaplaincy services through internal communications, such as newsletters and intranet posts.

- Impact Reports: Publish impact reports that highlight key achievements, success stories, and data on the benefits of chaplaincy services.

- Recognition Events: Organize events to recognize and celebrate the successes of the chaplaincy program, involving employees and stakeholders.

Example Practice

Global Enterprises regularly communicates the successes and impact of its chaplaincy services through newsletters, impact reports, and recognition events, maintaining visibility and support for the program.

Challenges and Solutions in Securing Ongoing Support and Investment

1. Demonstrating Tangible Benefits

Definition and Importance

Demonstrating tangible benefits of chaplaincy services can be challenging but is essential for securing ongoing support and investment.

Challenges

- Intangible Benefits: Many benefits of chaplaincy services, such as improved morale and well-being, are intangible and difficult to measure.

- Quantifying Impact: Quantifying the impact of chaplaincy services on organizational outcomes requires robust data collection and analysis.

Solutions

- Proxy Measures: Use proxy measures, such as employee engagement scores and absenteeism rates, to quantify the impact of chaplaincy services.

- Mixed Methods: Combine quantitative and qualitative methods to capture both tangible and intangible benefits.

- Success Stories: Use success stories and case studies to illustrate the tangible benefits of chaplaincy services.

Example Practice

At Creative Minds Corp, the corporate chaplain uses proxy measures and a combination of quantitative and qualitative methods to demonstrate the tangible benefits of chaplaincy services.

2. Addressing Budget Constraints

Definition and Importance

Addressing budget constraints is essential for securing ongoing investment in chaplaincy services, especially in challenging economic times.

Challenges

- Limited Resources: Organizations may face budget constraints that limit the availability of resources for chaplaincy services.

- Cost Justification: Justifying the cost of chaplaincy services requires clear evidence of their financial and operational benefits.

Solutions

- Cost-Benefit Analysis: Conduct a cost-benefit analysis to demonstrate the financial benefits of chaplaincy services, such as reduced turnover and healthcare costs.

- Flexible Budgeting: Propose flexible budgeting options that allow for scaling services based on available resources.

- Alternative Funding: Explore alternative funding sources, such as grants or partnerships, to supplement the budget for chaplaincy services.

Example Practice

Global Enterprises conducts a cost-benefit analysis and proposes flexible budgeting options to address budget constraints and secure ongoing investment in chaplaincy services.

Conclusion

Building the case for ongoing support and investment in chaplaincy services involves presenting comprehensive data and evidence, highlighting ROI, aligning with organizational goals and values, engaging key stakeholders, and regularly communicating successes and impact. Addressing challenges such as demonstrating tangible benefits and addressing budget constraints is crucial for securing the necessary resources and support. By effectively demonstrating the value of chaplaincy services, organizations can ensure the sustainability and growth of these programs, creating a supportive and positive workplace culture where employees feel valued and supported.

As we continue to explore the role of corporate chaplaincy in this book, we will delve into further strategies and best practices for addressing the common issues faced by employees. By understanding and addressing these challenges, organizations can create environments where employees feel valued, supported, and inspired.

CHAPTER 08

PERSONAL DEVELOPMENT FOR CHAPLAINS

Self-Care and Burnout Prevention

The Importance of Self-Care for Chaplains

Introduction

Chaplains provide invaluable support to employees, offering spiritual and emotional guidance in times of need. However, the nature of this work can be emotionally and mentally taxing, leading to burnout if self-care is neglected. This chapter emphasizes the importance of self-care for chaplains, exploring strategies to prevent burnout and maintain personal well-being.

Understanding Self-Care

1. Definition of Self-Care

Definition and Importance

Self-care involves engaging in activities and practices that maintain and improve one's physical, mental, and emotional well-being. For chaplains, self-care is essential for sustaining the energy and compassion required to support others effectively.

Impact

- Personal Well-Being: Enhances overall health and well-being.

- Professional Effectiveness: Ensures that chaplains can provide high-quality care to others.

- Resilience: Builds resilience, enabling chaplains to cope with the demands of their role.

Example

At Global Enterprises, chaplains who prioritize self-care report higher levels of job satisfaction and resilience, enabling them to support employees more effectively.

2. Components of Self-Care

Definition and Importance

Self-care encompasses various dimensions, including physical, emotional, mental, and spiritual well-being. Each component is crucial for maintaining balance and preventing burnout.

Impact

- Holistic Health: Promotes a holistic approach to health, addressing all aspects of well-being.

- Sustainable Practices: Encourages sustainable practices that support long-term health and resilience.

- Comprehensive Care: Ensures comprehensive self-care, addressing all areas of need.

Example

Wellness Tech Ltd. promotes a holistic approach to self-care for its chaplains, incorporating physical, emotional, mental, and spiritual practices into their routines.

Strategies for Effective Self-Care

1. Physical Self-Care

Definition and Importance

Physical self-care involves activities that promote physical health and well-being, such as exercise, nutrition, and adequate rest.

Implementation

- Regular Exercise: Engage in regular physical activity, such as walking, running, yoga, or strength training.

- Balanced Nutrition: Maintain a balanced diet that includes a variety of nutritious foods.

- Adequate Rest: Ensure adequate sleep and take breaks to rest and recharge during the day.

Example Practice

At Creative Minds Corp, chaplains are encouraged to participate in regular exercise programs and maintain balanced nutrition to support their physical health.

2. Emotional Self-Care

Definition and Importance

Emotional self-care involves activities that help manage and express emotions healthily and constructively.

Implementation

- Emotional Expression: Engage in activities that allow for healthy emotional expression, such as journaling, talking to a friend, or seeking therapy.

- Stress Management: Practice stress management techniques, such as deep breathing, meditation, or mindfulness.

- Boundaries: Set and maintain healthy boundaries to prevent emotional overload and burnout.

Example Practice

Global Enterprises provides resources for emotional self-care, including access to counseling services and stress management workshops for chaplains.

3. Mental Self-Care

Definition and Importance

Mental self-care involves activities that stimulate and engage the mind, promoting mental well-being and cognitive health.

Implementation

- Continued Learning: Engage in continued learning and professional development to stimulate the mind and enhance skills.

- Hobbies and Interests: Pursue hobbies and interests that provide mental stimulation and relaxation.

- Mindfulness Practices: Incorporate mindfulness practices into daily routines to enhance focus and mental clarity.

Example Practice

Wellness Tech Ltd. encourages chaplains to engage in continued learning and pursue hobbies, offering access to educational resources and mindfulness programs.

4. Spiritual Self-Care

Definition and Importance

Spiritual self-care involves activities that nurture the spirit and provide a sense of purpose and connection.

Implementation

- Personal Reflection: Engage in personal reflection and spiritual practices, such as prayer, meditation, or reading inspirational texts.

- Community Engagement: Participate in spiritual or religious communities for support and connection.

- Nature and Solitude: Spend time in nature and solitude to connect with the spiritual self and find peace.

Example Practice

At Creative Minds Corp, chaplains are encouraged to participate in spiritual practices and community engagement, fostering a sense of connection and purpose.

Preventing Burnout

1. Recognizing the Signs of Burnout

Definition and Importance

Recognizing the signs of burnout is the first step in addressing and preventing it. Burnout can manifest as physical, emotional, and mental exhaustion, reduced performance, and a sense of detachment.

Implementation

- Awareness: Develop awareness of common signs of burnout, such as chronic fatigue, irritability, and a sense of being overwhelmed.

- Self-Monitoring: Regularly self-monitor for signs of burnout and take action when needed.

- Peer Support: Encourage peer support among chaplains to recognize and address signs of burnout in each other.

Example Practice

Global Enterprises trains chaplains to recognize the signs of burnout and encourages peer support networks to provide mutual assistance and early intervention.

2. Developing a Burnout Prevention Plan

Definition and Importance

A burnout prevention plan outlines strategies and practices to maintain well-being and prevent burnout.

Implementation

- Personal Plan: Develop a personalized burnout prevention plan that includes strategies for physical, emotional, mental, and spiritual self-care.

- Regular Review: Regularly review and adjust the plan to ensure it remains effective and relevant.

- Professional Support: Seek professional support, such as counseling or supervision, to address challenges and prevent burnout.

Example Practice

Wellness Tech Ltd. encourages chaplains to develop personalized burnout prevention plans and provides access to professional support to ensure their effectiveness.

3. Maintaining Work-Life Balance

Definition and Importance

Maintaining a healthy work-life balance is crucial for preventing burnout and sustaining long-term well-being.

Implementation

- Time Management: Practice effective time management to balance work responsibilities and personal life.

- Setting Boundaries: Set clear boundaries between work and personal life to prevent overwork and ensure adequate rest.

- Leisure and Recreation: Prioritize leisure and recreational activities that provide relaxation and enjoyment.

Example Practice

At Creative Minds Corp, chaplains are encouraged to maintain a healthy work-life balance, with policies that support flexible working hours and promote leisure and recreational activities.

Challenges and Solutions in Practicing Self-Care

1. Overcoming Guilt and Self-Neglect

Definition and Importance

Chaplains may feel guilty about prioritizing self-care, leading to self-neglect and increased risk of burnout.

Challenges

- Guilt: Feelings of guilt about taking time for self-care.

- Self-Neglect: Neglecting self-care due to a focus on helping others.

Solutions

- Mindset Shift: Encourage a mindset shift that views self-care as essential for effective caregiving.

- Education: Provide education on the importance of self-care for maintaining personal well-being and professional effectiveness.

- Support Systems: Develop support systems that encourage and normalize self-care practices among chaplains.

Example Practice

Global Enterprises provides education and support systems to help chaplains overcome guilt and prioritize self-care, fostering a culture that values well-being.

2. Finding Time for Self-Care

Definition and Importance

Finding time for self-care can be challenging due to the demands of the chaplaincy role, but it is essential for sustaining well-being.

Challenges

- Busy Schedules: Demanding schedules that leave little time for self-care.

- Competing Priorities: Balancing self-care with professional and personal responsibilities.

Solutions

- Scheduled Self-Care: Schedule dedicated time for self-care activities in daily and weekly routines.

- Time Management: Use effective time management strategies to balance competing priorities and make time for self-care.

- Micro Self-Care: Incorporate micro self-care practices, such as short breaks and mindfulness exercises, into the workday.

Example Practice

Wellness Tech Ltd. encourages chaplains to schedule self-care activities and use time management strategies to balance their responsibilities, ensuring they find time for self-care.

Conclusion

Self-care is essential for chaplains to maintain their well-being and prevent burnout. By prioritizing physical, emotional, mental, and spiritual self-care, chaplains can sustain the energy and compassion needed to support others effectively. Recognizing the signs of burnout, developing a burnout prevention plan, and maintaining a healthy work-life balance are crucial strategies for preventing burnout. Addressing challenges such as overcoming guilt and finding time for self-care is essential for fostering a culture that values and supports well-being.

As we continue to explore the role of corporate chaplaincy in this book, we will delve into further strategies and best practices for addressing the common issues faced by chaplains. By understanding and addressing these challenges, organizations can create environments where chaplains feel valued, supported, and inspired.

Techniques for Managing Stress and Avoiding Burnout

Introduction

The demanding nature of chaplaincy work can lead to high levels of stress and potential burnout. Managing stress effectively and implementing strategies to avoid burnout are essential for maintaining personal well-being and professional effectiveness. This chapter explores various techniques that chaplains can use to manage stress and prevent burnout, ensuring they remain resilient and capable in their roles.

Understanding Stress and Burnout

1. Definition of Stress and Burnout

Definition and Importance

Stress is a physical, mental, and emotional response to demanding situations, while burnout is a state of chronic stress that leads to physical and emotional exhaustion, cynicism, and reduced professional efficacy.

Impact

- Stress: Can lead to short-term and long-term health issues, including anxiety, depression, and cardiovascular problems.

- Burnout: Results in decreased job performance, emotional exhaustion, and a sense of detachment from work.

Example

At Global Enterprises, chaplains are educated on the definitions and impacts of stress and burnout, helping them recognize these conditions early and take preventive actions.

Techniques for Managing Stress

1. Mindfulness and Meditation

Definition and Importance

Mindfulness and meditation involve focusing on the present moment and cultivating a state of awareness and acceptance. These practices are effective for reducing stress and promoting emotional well-being.

Implementation

- Mindfulness Exercises: Engage in daily mindfulness exercises, such as deep breathing, body scans, or mindful walking.

- Meditation Practices: Incorporate meditation practices into your routine, such as guided meditation, silent meditation, or loving-kindness meditation.

- Mindfulness Apps: Use mindfulness apps and online resources to support and guide your practice.

Example Practice

At Creative Minds Corp, chaplains participate in daily mindfulness exercises and use meditation apps to manage stress and enhance their emotional well-being.

2. Time Management Techniques

Definition and Importance

Effective time management helps reduce stress by organizing tasks, setting priorities, and ensuring a balanced workload.

Implementation

- Prioritization: Prioritize tasks based on their importance and urgency, focusing on high-priority activities first.

- Scheduling: Create a daily and weekly schedule to allocate time for work tasks, self-care, and leisure activities.

- Breaks: Incorporate regular breaks into your schedule to rest and recharge, preventing mental fatigue.

Example Practice

Global Enterprises provides time management training for chaplains, helping them prioritize tasks and create balanced schedules that include regular breaks.

3. Physical Activity

Definition and Importance

Regular physical activity is a proven way to reduce stress, improve mood, and enhance overall well-being.

Implementation

- Exercise Routine: Establish a regular exercise routine that includes activities you enjoy, such as walking, running, swimming, or yoga.

- Active Breaks: Take short active breaks during the day to stretch, walk, or engage in light physical activity.

- Group Activities: Participate in group exercise classes or sports to combine physical activity with social interaction.

Example Practice

Wellness Tech Ltd. encourages chaplains to maintain regular exercise routines and offers group exercise classes to promote physical activity and social connection.

4. Healthy Eating

Definition and Importance

Maintaining a healthy diet supports physical and mental health, helping to reduce stress and improve energy levels.

Implementation

- Balanced Diet: Eat a balanced diet that includes a variety of fruits, vegetables, whole grains, lean proteins, and healthy fats.

- Regular Meals: Avoid skipping meals and aim for regular meal times to maintain stable energy levels throughout the day.

- Hydration: Stay hydrated by drinking plenty of water and limiting caffeine and sugary drinks.

Example Practice

At Creative Minds Corp, chaplains are encouraged to maintain healthy eating habits and have access to nutritious food options in the workplace.

5. Social Support

Definition and Importance

Social support from friends, family, and colleagues provides emotional support, reduces feelings of isolation, and helps manage stress.

Implementation

- Support Network: Build and maintain a support network of friends, family, and colleagues you can turn to for emotional support.

- Peer Groups: Participate in peer support groups or professional networks to share experiences and receive support from fellow chaplains.

- Communication: Foster open communication with your support network, sharing your experiences and seeking advice and encouragement.

Example Practice

Global Enterprises facilitates peer support groups for chaplains, providing a space for sharing experiences and receiving mutual support.

Techniques for Avoiding Burnout

1. Setting Boundaries

Definition and Importance

Setting clear boundaries between work and personal life helps prevent overwork and ensures time for rest and rejuvenation.

Implementation

- Work Hours: Establish and stick to designated work hours, avoiding work tasks outside these hours.

- Personal Time: Dedicate time for personal activities and self-care, ensuring a balance between work and personal life.

- Technology Boundaries: Limit the use of work-related technology outside of work hours to prevent constant connectivity and mental fatigue.

Example Practice

At Creative Minds Corp, chaplains are encouraged to set and maintain clear boundaries between work and personal life, supported by policies that promote work-life balance.

2. Professional Development

Definition and Importance

Engaging in professional development helps chaplains stay motivated, enhance their skills, and find renewed purpose in their work.

Implementation

- Continued Education: Participate in continued education and training programs to enhance your knowledge and skills.

- Mentorship: Seek mentorship from experienced chaplains or professionals in your field for guidance and support.

- Goal Setting: Set professional development goals to stay motivated and focused on your career growth.

Example Practice

Wellness Tech Ltd. offers continued education opportunities and mentorship programs for chaplains, promoting professional growth and motivation.

3. Regular Supervision and Counseling

Definition and Importance

Regular supervision and counseling provide professional support, helping chaplains process their experiences and manage the emotional demands of their work.

Implementation

- Supervision Sessions: Schedule regular supervision sessions with a qualified supervisor to discuss your experiences, challenges, and successes.

- Counseling Services: Access counseling services for professional support and guidance in managing emotional and mental health.

- Peer Support: Participate in peer supervision groups to share experiences and receive mutual support.

Example Practice

Global Enterprises provides regular supervision and access to counseling services for chaplains, ensuring they have the support needed to manage their work's emotional demands.

4. Mindfulness and Reflection

Definition and Importance

Mindfulness and reflection practices help chaplains stay present, manage stress, and gain insights into their personal and professional experiences.

Implementation

- Daily Reflection: Set aside time each day for personal reflection, considering your experiences, emotions, and thoughts.

- Mindfulness Practices: Incorporate mindfulness practices, such as meditation or mindful breathing, into your daily routine.

- Journaling: Keep a journal to document your reflections, insights, and personal growth.

Example Practice

At Creative Minds Corp, chaplains are encouraged to practice daily reflection and mindfulness, supported by workshops and resources on these techniques.

Challenges and Solutions in Managing Stress and Avoiding Burnout

1. Balancing Multiple Responsibilities

Definition and Importance

Balancing multiple responsibilities, such as work, family, and personal commitments, can be challenging and contribute to stress and burnout.

Challenges

- Time Constraints: Limited time to manage multiple responsibilities effectively.

- Overload: Feeling overwhelmed by competing demands.

Solutions

- Prioritization: Prioritize responsibilities based on importance and urgency, focusing on high-priority tasks first.

- Delegation: Delegate tasks when possible to reduce workload and focus on essential responsibilities.

- Time Management: Use time management techniques to balance responsibilities and ensure time for self-care.

Example Practice

Wellness Tech Ltd. provides training on time management and delegation, helping chaplains balance their responsibilities and reduce stress.

2. Maintaining Consistency in Self-Care

Definition and Importance

Maintaining consistency in self-care practices is essential for long-term well-being and preventing burnout.

Challenges

- Routine Disruptions: Life events and work demands can disrupt self-care routines.

- Motivation: Maintaining motivation for self-care practices over time.

Solutions

- Flexibility: Adapt self-care practices to fit changing circumstances and maintain flexibility in your routine.

- Support Systems: Develop support systems that encourage and reinforce consistent self-care practices.

- Goal Setting: Set realistic and achievable self-care goals to stay motivated and focused.

Example Practice

Global Enterprises encourages chaplains to maintain flexibility in their self-care routines and provides support systems to help them stay consistent and motivated.

Conclusion

Managing stress and avoiding burnout are crucial for chaplains to maintain their well-being and effectiveness in their roles. By implementing techniques such as mindfulness, time management, physical activity, healthy eating, social support, setting boundaries, professional development, regular supervision, and reflection, chaplains can effectively manage stress and prevent burnout. Addressing challenges such as balancing multiple responsibilities and maintaining consistency in self-care is essential for sustaining long-term well-being and professional resilience.

As we continue to explore the role of corporate chaplaincy in this book, we will delve into further strategies and best practices for addressing the common issues faced by chaplains. By understanding and addressing these challenges, organizations can create environments where chaplains feel valued, supported, and inspired.

Balancing Personal and Professional Responsibilities

Introduction

Chaplains often face the challenge of balancing their personal and professional responsibilities. The demands of supporting others can sometimes overshadow the need for self-care and personal commitments. Achieving a healthy balance is crucial for maintaining overall well-being and professional effectiveness. This chapter explores strategies for balancing personal and professional responsibilities, helping chaplains manage their workload while maintaining a fulfilling personal life.

Understanding the Importance of Balance

1. Definition of Balance

Definition and Importance

Balance involves effectively managing time and energy between professional duties and personal life to ensure well-being and satisfaction in both areas.

Impact

- Well-Being: Promotes physical, emotional, and mental health.

- Job Satisfaction: Increases job satisfaction and reduces the risk of burnout.

- Personal Fulfillment: Enhances personal fulfillment and happiness by allowing time for family, hobbies, and self-care.

Example

At Global Enterprises, chaplains who achieve a balance between their work and personal lives report higher levels of job satisfaction and personal well-being.

Strategies for Balancing Personal and Professional Responsibilities

1. Setting Priorities

Definition and Importance

Setting priorities involves identifying the most important tasks and responsibilities in both personal and professional areas and focusing on them.

Implementation

- Identify Priorities: List your personal and professional responsibilities and identify which ones are most important and time-sensitive.

- Focus on Key Tasks: Allocate time and energy to high-priority tasks first, ensuring that essential responsibilities are addressed.

- Reevaluate Regularly: Regularly reevaluate your priorities to adjust to changing circumstances and needs.

Example Practice

At Creative Minds Corp, chaplains are encouraged to identify their top priorities and focus on them, ensuring that both work and personal responsibilities are effectively managed.

2. Time Management

Definition and Importance

Effective time management helps chaplains allocate time for both professional duties and personal activities, ensuring that neither area is neglected.

Implementation

- Scheduling: Create a detailed schedule that includes work tasks, personal activities, and self-care.

- Time Blocks: Use time-blocking techniques to allocate specific periods for different activities, reducing the risk of overlap and overcommitment.

- Flexibility: Build flexibility into your schedule to accommodate unexpected events and changes.

Example Practice

Global Enterprises provides training on time management techniques, helping chaplains create balanced schedules that include time for both work and personal activities.

3. Setting Boundaries

Definition and Importance

Setting boundaries involves establishing clear limits between work and personal life to prevent overwork and ensure time for rest and personal activities.

Implementation

- Work Hours: Define specific work hours and avoid work tasks outside these hours.

- Personal Time: Dedicate specific times for personal activities and self-care, ensuring that work does not encroach on personal time.

- Technology Boundaries: Limit the use of work-related technology outside of work hours to prevent constant connectivity and mental fatigue.

Example Practice

At Creative Minds Corp, chaplains are encouraged to set and maintain clear boundaries between work and personal life, supported by policies that promote work-life balance.

4. Delegating Responsibilities

Definition and Importance

Delegating responsibilities involves assigning tasks to others to reduce your workload and focus on high-priority activities.

Implementation

- Identify Tasks: Identify tasks that can be delegated to others, such as administrative duties or routine tasks.

- Trust and Empower: Trust and empower others to take on delegated responsibilities, providing guidance and support as needed.

- Follow-up: Follow up on delegated tasks to ensure they are completed effectively and to provide feedback.

Example Practice

Global Enterprises encourages chaplains to delegate appropriate tasks to colleagues or support staff, reducing their workload and allowing them to focus on more critical responsibilities.

5. Practicing Self-Care

Definition and Importance

Practicing self-care involves engaging in activities that maintain and improve physical, emotional, and mental well-being.

Implementation

- Regular Exercise: Engage in regular physical activity, such as walking, running, yoga, or strength training.

- Healthy Eating: Maintain a balanced diet that includes a variety of nutritious foods.

- Adequate Rest: Ensure adequate sleep and take breaks to rest and recharge during the day.

- Emotional Support: Seek emotional support from friends, family, or professional counselors.

Example Practice

At Creative Minds Corp, chaplains are encouraged to prioritize self-care, with access to resources and programs that support their physical and emotional well-being.

Addressing Challenges in Balancing Responsibilities

1. Dealing with Overcommitment

Definition and Importance

Overcommitment occurs when chaplains take on more responsibilities than they can manage, leading to stress and burnout.

Challenges

- Time Constraints: Limited time to manage multiple responsibilities effectively.

- Stress: Increased stress and anxiety from trying to meet all commitments.

Solutions

- Assess Commitments: Regularly assess your commitments and identify areas where you can reduce or delegate tasks.

- Learn to Say No: Develop the ability to say no to additional responsibilities that exceed your capacity.

- Seek Support: Seek support from colleagues, supervisors, or family members to manage your workload.

Example Practice

Global Enterprises encourages chaplains to regularly assess their commitments and provides support systems to help them manage their workload effectively.

2. Managing Unexpected Events

Definition and Importance

Unexpected events can disrupt your schedule and make it difficult to balance responsibilities.

Challenges

- Disruptions: Unexpected events can disrupt your planned schedule and increase stress.

- Flexibility: Difficulty in adjusting to sudden changes in responsibilities.

Solutions

- Build Flexibility: Build flexibility into your schedule to accommodate unexpected events and changes.

- Prioritize Urgency: Focus on urgent tasks first and adjust your schedule as needed to address unexpected events.

- Stay Calm: Practice stress management techniques to stay calm and focused during disruptions.

Example Practice

Creative Minds Corp. encourages chaplains to build flexibility into their schedules and provides training on stress management techniques to handle unexpected events effectively.

Conclusion

Balancing personal and professional responsibilities is essential for chaplains to maintain their well-being and effectiveness in their roles. By setting priorities, managing time effectively, setting boundaries, delegating responsibilities, and practicing self-care, chaplains can achieve a healthy balance between work and personal life. Addressing challenges such as overcommitment and managing unexpected events is crucial for sustaining this balance. Organizations can support chaplains by providing resources, training, and support systems that promote work-life balance and overall well-being.

As we continue to explore the role of corporate chaplaincy in this book, we will delve into further strategies and best practices for addressing the common issues faced by chaplains. By understanding and addressing these challenges, organizations can create environments where chaplains feel valued, supported, and inspired.

Continuing Education and Growth

Opportunities for Professional Development

Introduction

Continuing education and professional growth are essential for chaplains to stay updated with best practices, enhance their skills, and remain effective in their roles. Engaging in professional development opportunities ensures that chaplains can provide high-quality support to employees while also fostering their personal and professional growth. This chapter explores various opportunities for professional development available to chaplains and the benefits of ongoing education.

The Importance of Continuing Education and Growth

1. Maintaining Competence

Definition and Importance

Maintaining competence involves staying current with developments in the field, and ensuring that chaplains have the knowledge and skills necessary to provide effective support.

Impact

- Quality of Care: Enhances the quality of care provided to employees.

- Professional Standards: Ensures adherence to professional standards and ethical guidelines.

- Credibility: Builds credibility and trust with employees and stakeholders.

Example

At Global Enterprises, chaplains who engage in continuing education are better equipped to address complex issues and provide high-quality support.

2. Enhancing Professional Skills

Definition and Importance

Enhancing professional skills involves developing new competencies and refining existing ones to improve performance and effectiveness.

Impact

- Skill Development: Develops new skills and enhances existing ones.

- Innovation: Encourages the adoption of innovative practices and approaches.

- Career Advancement: Supports career advancement and professional growth.

Example

Wellness Tech Ltd. chaplains who participate in skill development programs are more effective in their roles and often advance to higher positions within the organization.

Opportunities for Professional Development

1. Formal Education Programs

Definition and Importance

Formal education programs, such as degrees, diplomas, and certifications, provide structured learning opportunities that enhance knowledge and skills.

Implementation

- Degrees and Diplomas: Enroll in degree or diploma programs in fields such as theology, counseling, psychology, or social work.

- Certifications: Obtain certifications in specialized areas, such as grief counseling, crisis intervention, or pastoral care.

- Online Courses: Take advantage of online courses and programs that offer flexibility and convenience.

Example Practice

At Creative Minds Corp, chaplains are encouraged to pursue formal education programs, with financial support and flexible work arrangements to accommodate their studies.

2. Workshops and Seminars

Definition and Importance

Workshops and seminars provide opportunities for focused learning on specific topics, allowing chaplains to gain new insights and practical skills.

Implementation

- Professional Conferences: Attend professional conferences that offer workshops and seminars on various aspects of chaplaincy and related fields.

- In-House Training: Participate in in-house training programs organized by the organization, focusing on relevant topics and skills.

- External Workshops: Enroll in workshops and seminars offered by external organizations and professional associations.

Example Practice

Global Enterprises sponsors chaplains to attend professional conferences and external workshops, providing opportunities for focused learning and skill development.

3. Mentorship and Coaching

Definition and Importance

Mentorship and coaching provide personalized guidance and support from experienced professionals, helping chaplains develop their skills and navigate their careers.

Implementation

- Mentorship Programs: Participate in mentorship programs that pair less experienced chaplains with seasoned mentors for guidance and support.

- Coaching Sessions: Engage in coaching sessions with professional coaches to develop specific skills and achieve career goals.

- Peer Mentoring: Establish peer mentoring relationships with colleagues for mutual support and learning.

Example Practice

Wellness Tech Ltd. offers mentorship programs for chaplains, pairing them with experienced mentors who provide personalized guidance and support.

4. Professional Associations

Definition and Importance

Joining professional associations provides access to resources, networking opportunities, and professional development events.

Implementation

- Membership: Join professional associations related to chaplaincy, such as the Association of Professional Chaplains (APC) or the National Association of Catholic Chaplains (NACC).

- Networking: Participate in networking events, conferences, and seminars organized by professional associations.

- Resources: Utilize resources and publications offered by professional associations to stay updated with industry trends and best practices.

Example Practice

At Creative Minds Corp, chaplains are encouraged to join professional associations and participate in their events, enhancing their professional development and networking opportunities.

5. Online Learning Platforms

Definition and Importance

Online learning platforms offer flexible and accessible opportunities for continuing education, allowing chaplains to learn at their own pace.

Implementation

- Webinars: Attend webinars on relevant topics, offering insights from experts in the field.

- E-Learning Courses: Enroll in e-learning courses that cover various aspects of chaplaincy and related disciplines.

- Virtual Conferences: Participate in virtual conferences that provide access to workshops, seminars, and networking opportunities.

Example Practice

Global Enterprises provides access to online learning platforms, enabling chaplains to participate in webinars, e-learning courses, and virtual conferences for ongoing education.

Benefits of Continuing Education and Growth

1. Improved Job Performance

Definition and Importance

Continuing education enhances job performance by providing chaplains with up-to-date knowledge and skills, enabling them to perform their duties more effectively.

Impact

- Effective Support: Enables chaplains to provide more effective support to employees.

- Innovative Practices: Encourages the adoption of innovative practices and approaches.

- Professional Competence: Ensures that chaplains remain competent and effective in their roles.

Example

At Global Enterprises, chaplains who engage in continuing education report improved job performance and effectiveness in supporting employees.

2. Increased Job Satisfaction

Definition and Importance

Engaging in professional development contributes to increased job satisfaction by providing opportunities for personal and professional growth.

Impact

- Career Fulfillment: Enhances career fulfillment and motivation.

- Skill Development: Provides opportunities for skill development and career advancement.

- Personal Growth: Promotes personal growth and self-improvement.

Example

Wellness Tech Ltd. chaplains who participate in professional development programs report higher levels of job satisfaction and career fulfillment.

3. Enhanced Professional Network

Definition and Importance

Continuing education and participation in professional associations expand chaplains' professional networks, providing opportunities for collaboration and support.

Impact

- Networking: Expands professional networks and connections.

- Collaboration: Encourages collaboration and sharing of best practices.

- Support System: Provides a support system of peers and mentors.

Example

At Creative Minds Corp, chaplains who join professional associations and participate in networking events benefit from expanded professional networks and collaborative opportunities.

4. Staying Current with Best Practices

Definition and Importance

Continuing education ensures that chaplains stay current with best practices, industry trends, and new developments in the field.

Impact

- Up-to-Date Knowledge: Keeps chaplains informed about the latest developments and best practices.

- Quality of Care: Enhances the quality of care provided to employees.

- Professional Standards: Ensures adherence to professional standards and ethical guidelines.

Example

Global Enterprises supports chaplains in staying current with best practices through access to professional development resources and training programs.

Challenges and Solutions in Continuing Education and Growth

1. Time Constraints

Definition and Importance

Balancing continuing education with professional and personal responsibilities can be challenging due to time constraints.

Challenges

- Busy Schedules: Limited time to engage in continuing education due to busy work schedules.

- Competing Priorities: Balancing professional development with personal and professional responsibilities.

Solutions

- Flexible Learning: Utilize flexible learning options, such as online courses and webinars, that can be completed at your own pace.

- Time Management: Practice effective time management to allocate time for continuing education.

- Supportive Policies: Advocate for supportive policies that allow for dedicated time for professional development.

Example Practice

At Creative Minds Corp, chaplains are encouraged to use flexible learning options and receive support from the organization to balance continuing education with their responsibilities.

2. Financial Constraints

Definition and Importance

Financial constraints can limit access to professional development opportunities, such as courses, certifications, and conferences.

Challenges

- Cost of Education: High costs associated with continuing education programs and certifications.

- Limited Funding: Limited organizational funding for professional development.

Solutions

- Employer Support: Seek financial support from your employer for continuing education and professional development.

- Grants and Scholarships: Apply for grants and scholarships that support continuing education for chaplains.

- Low-Cost Options: Explore low-cost or free professional development options, such as online courses and webinars.

Example Practice

Global Enterprises provides financial support for chaplains to pursue continuing education and encourages them to apply for external grants and scholarships.

Conclusion

Continuing education and professional growth are essential for chaplains to maintain their competence, enhance their skills, and stay effective in their roles. By engaging in formal education programs, workshops, seminars, mentorship, professional associations, and online learning platforms, chaplains can pursue ongoing education and growth. The benefits of continuing education include improved job performance, increased job satisfaction, enhanced professional networks, and staying current with best practices. Addressing challenges such as time and financial constraints is crucial for ensuring access to professional development opportunities.

As we continue to explore the role of corporate chaplaincy in this book, we will delve into further strategies and best practices for addressing the common issues faced by chaplains. By understanding and addressing these challenges, organizations can create environments where chaplains feel valued, supported, and inspired.

Networking with Other Chaplains and Spiritual Leaders

Introduction

Networking with other chaplains and spiritual leaders is an essential aspect of professional development for chaplains. Building a network of peers provides opportunities for sharing experiences, learning from one another, and receiving mutual support. This chapter explores the importance of networking, strategies for building professional relationships, and the benefits of engaging with a broader community of spiritual leaders.

The Importance of Networking

1. Professional Growth

Definition and Importance

Networking with other chaplains and spiritual leaders fosters professional growth by providing opportunities for learning, collaboration, and sharing best practices.

Impact

- Knowledge Exchange: Facilitates the exchange of knowledge and ideas.

- Skill Enhancement: Enhances professional skills through shared experiences and learning.

- Career Advancement: Supports career advancement by expanding professional connections and opportunities.

Example

At Global Enterprises, chaplains who actively network with peers and spiritual leaders report significant professional growth and improved job performance.

2. Emotional and Professional Support

Definition and Importance

Networking provides emotional and professional support, helping chaplains navigate the challenges of their roles and prevent burnout.

Impact

- Peer Support: Offers a support system of peers who understand the unique challenges of chaplaincy.

- Mentorship: Provides access to mentors who can offer guidance and advice.

- Resilience: Builds resilience by fostering a sense of community and shared purpose.

Example

Wellness Tech Ltd. chaplains who engage in networking activities find emotional support and mentorship invaluable for managing stress and maintaining resilience.

Strategies for Networking

1. Joining Professional Associations

Definition and Importance

Professional associations offer structured opportunities for networking, professional development, and access to resources.

Implementation

- Membership: Join relevant professional associations, such as the Association of Professional Chaplains (APC) or the National Association of Catholic Chaplains (NACC).

- Participation: Actively participate in association events, such as conferences, workshops, and webinars.

- Volunteering: Volunteer for committees or leadership roles within the association to increase visibility and engagement.

Example Practice

At Creative Minds Corp, chaplains are encouraged to join and actively participate in professional associations, enhancing their networking opportunities and professional development.

2. Attending Conferences and Workshops

Definition and Importance

Conferences and workshops provide opportunities to meet other chaplains and spiritual leaders, exchange ideas, and learn about new developments in the field.

Implementation

- Conference Attendance: Attend regional, national, and international conferences related to chaplaincy and spiritual care.

- Workshop Participation: Participate in workshops that focus on specific areas of interest or skill development.

- Networking Sessions: Take advantage of networking sessions and social events at conferences to connect with peers.

Example Practice

Global Enterprises supports chaplains in attending conferences and workshops, providing funding and time off to participate in these professional development opportunities.

3. Engaging in Online Communities

Definition and Importance

Online communities offer a flexible and accessible way to network with other chaplains and spiritual leaders, regardless of geographic location.

Implementation

- Social Media Groups: Join social media groups and online forums dedicated to chaplaincy and spiritual care.

- Professional Networks: Engage with professional networks on platforms like LinkedIn to connect with other chaplains and spiritual leaders.

- Webinars and Virtual Meetings: Participate in webinars, virtual conferences, and online meetings to interact with peers and learn from experts.

Example Practice

Wellness Tech Ltd. chaplains participate in online communities and virtual events, expanding their professional networks and accessing diverse perspectives and resources.

4. Participating in Local and Regional Networks

Definition and Importance

Local and regional networks provide opportunities for face-to-face interaction and collaboration with nearby chaplains and spiritual leaders.

Implementation

- Local Chapters: Join local chapters of professional associations or community organizations focused on spiritual care.

- Regional Events: Attend regional events, such as workshops, seminars, and retreats, to meet and collaborate with nearby peers.

- Interfaith Groups: Participate in interfaith groups and coalitions to build relationships with spiritual leaders from different traditions.

Example Practice

At Creative Minds Corp, chaplains are encouraged to participate in local and regional networks, fostering connections and collaboration with nearby peers.

Benefits of Networking with Other Chaplains and Spiritual Leaders

1. Knowledge Sharing and Collaboration

Definition and Importance

Networking facilitates knowledge sharing and collaboration, enabling chaplains to learn from one another and work together on common goals.

Impact

- Best Practices: Share and learn best practices for providing effective spiritual care.

- Collaborative Projects: Engage in collaborative projects and initiatives that benefit the broader community.

- Innovative Solutions: Develop innovative solutions to common challenges through collective brainstorming and problem-solving.

Example

Global Enterprise's chaplains who engage in networking activities report learning new techniques and approaches from their peers, enhancing their effectiveness in their roles.

2. Professional Development and Growth

Definition and Importance

Networking supports professional development and growth by providing access to resources, mentorship, and career advancement opportunities.

Impact

- Career Opportunities: Access job openings, promotions, and career advancement opportunities through professional connections.

- Mentorship: Receive mentorship and guidance from experienced chaplains and spiritual leaders.

- Educational Resources: Gain access to educational resources, training programs, and professional development opportunities.

Example

Wellness Tech Ltd. chaplains who actively network with peers and mentors report significant professional growth and career advancement.

3. Emotional and Spiritual Support

Definition and Importance

Networking provides emotional and spiritual support, helping chaplains cope with the emotional demands of their work and maintain their well-being.

Impact

- Peer Support: Receive emotional support and encouragement from peers who understand the challenges of chaplaincy.

- Spiritual Nourishment: Engage in spiritual practices and discussions with other spiritual leaders to nurture personal spirituality.

- Sense of Community: Foster a sense of community and belonging, reducing feelings of isolation and burnout.

Example

At Creative Minds Corp, chaplains who participate in networking activities find emotional and spiritual support invaluable for maintaining their well-being and resilience.

Challenges and Solutions in Networking

1. Overcoming Geographical Barriers

Definition and Importance

Geographical barriers can limit opportunities for face-to-face networking, especially for chaplains in remote or rural areas.

Challenges

- Limited Local Opportunities: Fewer local events and networks available.

- Travel Constraints: Difficulty attending distant conferences and events due to travel constraints.

Solutions

- Virtual Networking: Utilize online platforms and virtual events to connect with peers and spiritual leaders from different locations.

- Local Initiatives: Initiate or join local networking groups and events to build connections within your community.

- Collaborative Technologies: Use collaborative technologies, such as video conferencing and online forums, to facilitate remote networking.

Example Practice

Global Enterprises chaplains use virtual networking platforms and online events to connect with peers, overcoming geographical barriers and expanding their professional networks.

2. Balancing Networking with Other Responsibilities

Definition and Importance

Balancing networking activities with professional and personal responsibilities can be challenging, especially for chaplains with demanding schedules.

Challenges

- Time Constraints: Limited time to engage in networking activities due to busy work schedules.

- Competing Priorities: Balancing networking with other professional and personal commitments.

Solutions

- Scheduled Networking: Schedule dedicated time for networking activities, such as attending events or participating in online forums.

- Integrated Activities: Integrate networking with other professional development activities, such as attending conferences or workshops.

- Supportive Policies: Advocate for supportive organizational policies that allow time for professional networking.

Example Practice

Wellness Tech Ltd. supports chaplains by providing time and resources for networking activities, ensuring they can balance networking with their other responsibilities.

Conclusion

Networking with other chaplains and spiritual leaders is essential for professional development, emotional support, and career growth. By joining professional associations, attending conferences and workshops, engaging in online communities, and participating in local and regional networks, chaplains can build a robust professional network. The benefits of networking include knowledge sharing, collaboration, professional development, and emotional support. Addressing challenges such as geographical barriers and balancing networking with other responsibilities is crucial for effective networking.

As we continue to explore the role of corporate chaplaincy in this book, we will delve into further strategies and best practices for addressing the common issues faced by chaplains. By understanding and addressing these challenges, organizations can create environments where chaplains feel valued, supported, and inspired.

Staying Updated with the Latest Research and Practices

Introduction

In the dynamic field of chaplaincy, staying updated with the latest research and practices is crucial for providing high-quality care and support to employees. Keeping abreast of new developments, methodologies, and best practices ensures that chaplains can offer effective, evidence-based interventions and maintain professional competence. This chapter explores strategies for staying informed about the latest research and practices in chaplaincy and related fields.

The Importance of Staying Updated

1. Enhancing Professional Competence

Definition and Importance

Staying updated with the latest research and practices ensures that chaplains maintain their professional competence and deliver high-quality care.

Impact

- Evidence-Based Practice: Incorporates the latest evidence into practice, enhancing the effectiveness of interventions.

- Professional Standards: Ensures adherence to current professional standards and guidelines.

- Credibility: Builds credibility and trust with employees and stakeholders by demonstrating a commitment to professional excellence.

Example

At Global Enterprises, chaplains who stay informed about the latest research report higher confidence in their abilities and improved care outcomes.

2. Improving Care Quality

Definition and Importance

Keeping up with new developments and best practices improves the quality of care provided to employees, addressing their evolving needs more effectively.

Impact

- Innovative Approaches: Introduces innovative approaches and techniques that enhance care quality.

- Adaptability: Enhances adaptability to new challenges and changing employee needs.

- Comprehensive Care: Ensures that care is comprehensive and aligned with the latest standards in the field.

Example

Wellness Tech Ltd. chaplains who integrate the latest research into their practice provide more comprehensive and effective care to employees.

Strategies for Staying Updated

1. Engaging with Professional Associations

Definition and Importance

Professional associations offer access to the latest research, publications, and best practices in the field of chaplaincy and spiritual care.

Implementation

- Membership: Join relevant professional associations, such as the Association of Professional Chaplains (APC) or the National Association of Catholic Chaplains (NACC).

- Publications: Subscribe to journals, newsletters, and publications offered by these associations.

- Events and Conferences: Attend events, conferences, and webinars organized by professional associations to stay informed about the latest developments.

Example Practice

At Creative Minds Corp, chaplains are encouraged to join professional associations and actively engage with their resources and events to stay updated.

2. Participating in Continuing Education

Definition and Importance

Continuing education programs provide structured opportunities for learning about the latest research and practices in chaplaincy and related fields.

Implementation

- Online Courses: Enroll in online courses and webinars that focus on current research and best practices.

- Workshops and Seminars: Attend workshops and seminars that provide in-depth insights into specific topics.

- Certifications: Pursue certifications in specialized areas to deepen knowledge and skills.

Example Practice

Global Enterprises supports chaplains in participating in continuing education programs, offering funding and time off to pursue these opportunities.

3. Reading Peer-Reviewed Journals and Publications

Definition and Importance

Reading peer-reviewed journals and publications helps chaplains stay informed about the latest research findings and theoretical developments.

Implementation

- Journal Subscriptions: Subscribe to leading journals in chaplaincy, theology, counseling, and related fields.

- Library Access: Utilize institutional library access to explore a wide range of academic publications.

- Regular Reading: Set aside regular time for reading and reviewing recent articles and studies.

Example Practice

Wellness Tech Ltd. provides chaplains with access to a library of peer-reviewed journals and encourages regular reading to stay informed about current research.

4. Networking with Researchers and Academics

Definition and Importance

Networking with researchers and academics in the field provides direct access to cutting-edge research and innovative practices.

Implementation

- Academic Conferences: Attend academic conferences and symposia to meet researchers and learn about their work.

- Collaborative Projects: Engage in collaborative projects and research initiatives with academic institutions.

- Discussion Groups: Join discussion groups and online forums where researchers and practitioners share insights and findings.

Example Practice

At Creative Minds Corp, chaplains are encouraged to network with researchers and participate in academic conferences to stay updated with the latest research.

5. Utilizing Online Resources and Databases

Definition and Importance

Online resources and databases provide easy access to a vast array of research articles, publications, and practice guidelines.

Implementation

- Research Databases: Use research databases such as PubMed, JSTOR, and Google Scholar to find relevant articles and studies.

- Professional Websites: Explore professional websites and online platforms that offer resources and guidelines for chaplains.

- E-Learning Platforms: Utilize e-learning platforms that provide courses, webinars, and resources on the latest practices.

Example Practice

Global Enterprises encourages chaplains to use online resources and databases, providing access to subscriptions and e-learning platforms to support their ongoing education.

Benefits of Staying Updated

1. Informed Decision-Making

Definition and Importance

Staying updated with the latest research and practices enables chaplains to make informed decisions about care interventions and support strategies.

Impact

- Evidence-Based Interventions: Ensures that interventions are based on the latest evidence and research findings.

- Effective Solutions: Facilitates the implementation of effective solutions to complex challenges.

- Continuous Improvement: Promotes continuous improvement in care quality and outcomes.

Example

At Global Enterprises, chaplains who stay informed about the latest research reports make more informed and effective decisions in their practice.

2. Professional Development and Growth

Definition and Importance

Engaging with the latest research and practices contributes to ongoing professional development and growth, enhancing career satisfaction and advancement opportunities.

Impact

- Skill Enhancement: Enhances professional skills and competencies.

- Career Advancement: Supports career advancement and opportunities for leadership roles.

- Lifelong Learning: Fosters a culture of lifelong learning and professional excellence.

Example

Wellness Tech Ltd. chaplains who actively engage with current research and best practices report higher levels of job satisfaction and career growth.

3. Enhanced Care Quality

Definition and Importance

Staying updated with the latest research and practices improves the quality of care provided to employees, ensuring that support is effective and aligned with current standards.

Impact

- Innovative Practices: Incorporates innovative practices and techniques that enhance care quality.

- Adaptability: Enhances adaptability to new challenges and changing employee needs.

- Comprehensive Support: Ensures that support is comprehensive and evidence-based.

Example

At Crative Minds Corp, chaplains who stay informed about the latest research and practices provide higher-quality, more effective care to employees.

Challenges and Solutions in Staying Updated

1. Time Constraints

Definition and Importance

Balancing the demands of staying updated with other professional and personal responsibilities can be challenging due to time constraints.

Challenges

- Busy Schedules: Limited time to engage in continuing education and research activities.

- Competing Priorities: Balancing ongoing education with professional and personal commitments.

Solutions

- Time Management: Practice effective time management to allocate time for staying updated.

- Flexible Learning: Utilize flexible learning options, such as online courses and webinars, that fit into busy schedules.

- Scheduled Reading: Set aside dedicated time each week for reading and engaging with current research.

Example Practice

Global Enterprises encourages chaplains to practice time management and provides flexible learning options to help them stay updated despite busy schedules.

2. Access to Resources

Definition and Importance

Access to the latest research and publications can be limited due to financial constraints or lack of institutional support.

Challenges

- Cost of Subscriptions: High costs associated with journal subscriptions and continuing education programs.

- Limited Access: Lack of access to institutional libraries and resources.

Solutions

- Employer Support: Seek financial support from employers for journal subscriptions and continuing education.

- Open Access: Utilize open-access journals and free online resources.

- Collaborative Access: Partner with academic institutions or libraries for access to research databases and publications.

Example Practice

Wellness Tech Ltd. provides financial support and access to institutional resources for chaplains, ensuring they have the necessary tools to stay updated.

Conclusion

Staying updated with the latest research and practices is essential for chaplains to maintain professional competence, enhance care quality, and support ongoing professional growth. By engaging with professional associations, participating in continuing education, reading peer-reviewed journals, networking with researchers, and utilizing online resources, chaplains can stay informed about current developments in the field. Addressing challenges such as time constraints and access to resources is crucial for effective ongoing education. Organizations can support chaplains by providing resources, funding, and opportunities for professional development.

As we continue to explore the role of corporate chaplaincy in this book, we will delve into further strategies and best practices for addressing the common issues faced by chaplains. By understanding and addressing these challenges, organizations can create environments where chaplains feel valued, supported, and inspired.

384

RESOURCES FOR CORPORATE CHAPLAINS

Recommended Readings and Resources

Introduction

Staying informed and continually developing professional skills is essential for corporate chaplains. This appendix provides a curated list of recommended readings and resources that can support chaplains in their professional growth, offering insights into the latest research, best practices, and practical tools for effective chaplaincy.

Books

1. "The Practice of Pastoral Care: A Postmodern Approach" by Carrie Doehring

   - Provides a comprehensive guide to pastoral care in contemporary contexts, integrating theory and practice with a focus on cultural sensitivity and ethical practice.

2. "Professional Spiritual & Pastoral Care: A Practical Clergy and Chaplain's Handbook" edited by Stephen B. Roberts

- A thorough resource offering practical guidance for chaplains and clergy in various settings, covering a wide range of topics from crisis intervention to self-care.

3. "Spiritual Care in Practice: Case Studies in Healthcare Chaplaincy" edited by George Fitchett and Steve Nolan

- This collection of case studies explores the practical aspects of spiritual care, providing insights into real-world applications and best practices.

4. "The Wounded Healer: Ministry in Contemporary Society" by Henri J.M. Nouwen

- Explores the concept of the wounded healer, offering profound reflections on the role of chaplains and the importance of self-awareness and personal growth.

5. "A Ministry of Presence: Chaplaincy, Spiritual Care, and the Law" by Winnifred Fallers Sullivan

- Examines the legal and institutional challenges of chaplaincy work, providing a thoughtful analysis of the role of chaplains in various contexts.

6. "Soul Care: Christian Faith and Academic Administration" by Harold G. Koenig

- Focuses on the integration of spiritual care in academic settings, offering valuable insights for chaplains working in educational institutions.

7. "The Art of Listening in the Healing Process" by Jeanne Denney

- Emphasizes the importance of listening in spiritual care, providing practical techniques and insights for effective pastoral counseling.

Journals and Publications

1. Journal of Pastoral Care & Counseling (JPCC)

- A leading peer-reviewed journal that publishes research, case studies, and best practices in pastoral care and counseling.

2. Journal of Health Care Chaplaincy

- Focuses on the role of chaplaincy in healthcare settings, offering research articles and practical insights for chaplains working in hospitals and clinics.

3. The Journal of Pastoral Psychology

- Explores the intersection of psychology and pastoral care, providing research and theoretical articles on various aspects of spiritual and emotional well-being.

4. Health and Social Care Chaplaincy

- A journal dedicated to the practice and research of chaplaincy in health and social care, offering a range of articles on practical and theoretical topics.

Professional Associations and Organizations

1. Association of Professional Chaplains (APC)

- A professional organization that offers certification, education, and resources for chaplains across various settings. (Website: www.professionalchaplains.org)

2. National Association of Catholic Chaplains (NACC)

- Provides certification, education, and networking opportunities for Catholic chaplains. (Website: www.nacc.org)

3. National Association of Jewish Chaplains (NAJC)

- Offers resources, certification, and support for Jewish chaplains. (Website: www.najc.org)

4. Spiritual Care Association (SCA)

- An organization that provides education, certification, and resources for chaplains and spiritual care providers. (Website: www.spiritualcareassociation.org)

5. College of Pastoral Supervision and Psychotherapy (CPSP)

- Focuses on the certification and support of pastoral supervisors and psychotherapists, offering resources for professional growth. (Website: www.cpsp.org)

Online Resources and Learning Platforms

1. Chaplaincy Innovation Lab

- An online resource that offers webinars, articles, and research on innovative practices in chaplaincy. (Website: www.chaplaincyinnovation.org)

2. Spiritual Care Association Learning Center

- Provides a variety of online courses and webinars on topics related to spiritual care and chaplaincy. (Website: www.spiritualcareassociation.org/learning-center.html)

3. Coursera

- Offers a range of online courses from leading universities on topics related to counseling, psychology, and spiritual care. (Website: www.coursera.org)

4. edX

- An online learning platform that provides courses from top universities on various subjects, including mental health, counseling, and spirituality. (Website: www.edx.org)

5. LinkedIn Learning

- Offers a wide range of professional development courses, including those focused on leadership, communication, and emotional intelligence. (Website: www.linkedin.com/learning)

Research Databases

1. PubMed

- A free database of medical and psychological research articles, including those related to pastoral care and chaplaincy. (Website: www.pubmed.gov)

2. JSTOR

- Provides access to a wide range of academic journals and articles, including those in theology, psychology, and counseling. (Website: www.jstor.org)

3. Google Scholar

- A freely accessible search engine that indexes scholarly articles across various disciplines, including chaplaincy and spiritual care. (Website: scholar.google.com)

4. PsycINFO

- A database of psychological literature that includes research articles on counseling, therapy, and mental health. (Access through institutional subscriptions)

Conclusion

These recommended readings and resources provide a solid foundation for corporate chaplains seeking to enhance their knowledge, skills, and professional development. By engaging with these materials and organizations, chaplains can stay informed about the latest research and best practices, ensuring they provide high-quality, evidence-based care to employees. Continuous learning and professional growth are essential for maintaining excellence in chaplaincy, and these resources offer valuable support in achieving that goal.

Dr. Maxwell Shimba

APPENDIX

PROFESSIONAL ORGANIZATIONS AND NETWORKS

Appendix: Resources for Corporate Chaplains

Professional Organizations and Networks

Introduction

Joining professional organizations and networks is crucial for corporate chaplains seeking to enhance their professional development, stay informed about the latest research and practices, and connect with peers in the field. These organizations provide valuable resources, educational opportunities, and support systems that help chaplains excel in their roles. This section provides a list of key professional organizations and networks that corporate chaplains can join to advance their careers and enrich their practice.

Professional Organizations

1. Association of Professional Chaplains (APC)

- Overview: APC is a leading professional organization that certifies and supports chaplains in various settings, including healthcare, military, correctional facilities, and more.

- Benefits: Certification, continuing education, professional development resources, annual conferences, and networking opportunities.

- Website: www.professionalchaplains.org

2. National Association of Catholic Chaplains (NACC)

- Overview: NACC provides certification, education, and support for Catholic chaplains serving in healthcare, prisons, universities, and other settings.

- Benefits: Certification, educational resources, professional support, annual conferences, and networking opportunities.

- Website: www.nacc.org

3. National Association of Jewish Chaplains (NAJC)

- Overview: NAJC offers certification, professional development, and support for Jewish chaplains working in diverse environments.

- Benefits: Certification, professional development programs, conferences, publications, and networking.

- Website: www.najc.org

4. Spiritual Care Association (SCA)

- Overview: SCA provides education, certification, and resources for chaplains and spiritual care providers across various settings.

- Benefits: Certification, online learning resources, professional development, research, and networking opportunities.

- Website: www.spiritualcareassociation.org

5. College of Pastoral Supervision and Psychotherapy (CPSP)

- Overview: CPSP focuses on the certification and support of pastoral supervisors and psychotherapists, promoting high standards in pastoral care and counseling.

- Benefits: Certification, continuing education, peer support, conferences, and professional development.

- Website: www.cpsp.org

6. Healthcare Chaplains Ministry Association (HCMA)

- Overview: HCMA provides support and resources for chaplains serving in healthcare settings, promoting excellence in spiritual care.

- Benefits: Certification, professional development, publications, and networking opportunities.

- Website: www.healthcarechaplains.org

7. Military Chaplains Association (MCA)

- Overview: MCA supports chaplains serving in the military, providing resources, advocacy, and professional development.

- Benefits: Professional support, educational resources, conferences, and networking opportunities.

- Website: www.mca-usa.org

8. American Association of Pastoral Counselors (AAPC)

- Overview: AAPC offers resources and support for pastoral counselors, integrating spiritual and psychological care.

- Benefits: Certification, continuing education, professional development, and networking.

- Website: www.aapc.org

Networking Opportunities

1. Local and Regional Chaplaincy Networks

- Overview: Local and regional networks provide opportunities for chaplains to connect with peers in their area, share experiences, and collaborate on projects.

- Benefits: Peer support, professional development, local conferences, and collaborative initiatives.

2. Online Professional Networks

- LinkedIn Groups: Join LinkedIn groups related to chaplaincy and spiritual care to connect with professionals, share resources, and engage in discussions.

- Example Groups: "Healthcare Chaplaincy," "Professional Chaplains Network," "Spiritual Care Professionals."

- Social Media: Follow professional organizations and thought leaders on platforms like Twitter and Facebook to stay updated on news, events, and discussions.

3. Professional Conferences and Workshops

- Overview: Attend professional conferences and workshops organized by chaplaincy organizations to learn from experts, participate in training sessions, and network with peers.

- Benefits: Continuing education, exposure to new research and practices, and networking opportunities.

4. Mentorship Programs

- Overview: Participate in mentorship programs offered by professional organizations to receive guidance and support from experienced chaplains.

- Benefits: Personalized mentorship, professional growth, and career development.

Benefits of Joining Professional Organizations and Networks

1. Access to Resources and Education

- Description: Members gain access to a wealth of resources, including journals, publications, webinars, and online courses.

- Impact: Enhances professional knowledge and skills, keeping chaplains informed about the latest research and best practices.

2. Certification and Credentialing

- Description: Professional organizations offer certification and credentialing programs that validate a chaplain's expertise and commitment to high standards.

- Impact: Increases credibility, job opportunities, and professional recognition.

3. Professional Support and Advocacy

- Description: Organizations provide professional support and advocate for the interests of chaplains in various settings.

- Impact: Ensures that chaplains have the resources and support needed to perform their roles effectively.

4. Networking and Collaboration

- Description: Opportunities to network with peers, share experiences, and collaborate on projects and initiatives.

- Impact: Builds a supportive community, fosters collaboration, and enhances professional development.

Conclusion

Joining professional organizations and networks is a vital step for corporate chaplains seeking to enhance their professional development, stay informed about the latest research and practices, and connect with peers in the field. These organizations provide valuable resources, educational opportunities, certification, and support systems that help chaplains excel in their roles. By actively participating in these networks, chaplains can achieve continuous growth, improve their practice, and contribute to the advancement of the chaplaincy profession.

Dr. Maxwell Shimba

THE HUNT FOR GOLD

Appendix: Resources for Corporate Chaplains

Glossary of Terms

Introduction

Understanding key terms and concepts is essential for corporate chaplains to navigate their roles effectively and communicate clearly with colleagues and employees. This glossary provides definitions of important terms and concepts commonly used in corporate chaplaincy, offering a valuable reference for both new and experienced chaplains.

Glossary of Terms

1. Chaplain

   - Definition: A trained professional who provides spiritual, emotional, and pastoral care in various settings, including workplaces, hospitals, military, and educational institutions.

- Context: Corporate chaplains support employees by offering counseling, crisis intervention, and spiritual guidance.

2. Pastoral Care

- Definition: A form of emotional and spiritual support provided by chaplains or religious leaders to individuals in need.

- Context: Pastoral care includes activities such as counseling, prayer, and spiritual guidance.

3. Spiritual Care

- Definition: Support that addresses the spiritual and religious needs of individuals, helping them find meaning, purpose, and comfort.

- Context: Corporate chaplains provide spiritual care to employees regardless of their religious affiliation.

4. Emotional Support

- Definition: Assistance provided to help individuals cope with emotional distress, stress, or mental health challenges.

- Context: Chaplains offer emotional support through active listening, empathy, and counseling.

5. Crisis Intervention

- Definition: Immediate and short-term assistance provided to individuals experiencing a crisis, aiming to stabilize their situation and provide support.

- Context: Corporate chaplains are trained to respond to workplace crises, such as accidents or sudden losses.

6. Confidentiality

- Definition: The ethical principle of keeping information shared by individuals private and not disclosing it without their consent.

- Context: Chaplains maintain confidentiality to build trust and provide effective support.

7. Counseling

- Definition: A professional relationship that helps individuals resolve personal, social, or psychological issues and improve their well-being.

- Context: Corporate chaplains offer counseling to employees dealing with stress, grief, or other personal challenges.

8. Ethical Standards

- Definition: Guidelines that outline the professional conduct and ethical behavior expected of chaplains.

- Context: Chaplains adhere to ethical standards to ensure they provide care with integrity and respect.

9. Multifaith Chaplaincy

- Definition: A chaplaincy model that provides spiritual care to individuals of diverse religious backgrounds.

- Context: Corporate chaplains often serve in multifaith environments, respecting and addressing the spiritual needs of all employees.

10. Interfaith Dialogue

- Definition: Conversations and interactions between people of different religious traditions to promote understanding and cooperation.

- Context: Chaplains facilitate interfaith dialogue to foster a respectful and inclusive workplace culture.

11. Reflective Practice

- Definition: A method of self-assessment where chaplains reflect on their experiences and actions to improve their practice.

- Context: Reflective practice helps chaplains learn from their experiences and enhance their care.

12. Well-Being

- Definition: The state of being comfortable, healthy, and happy, encompassing physical, mental, and emotional health.

- Context: Corporate chaplains aim to promote the well-being of employees through holistic support.

13. Burnout

- Definition: A state of physical, emotional, and mental exhaustion caused by prolonged stress and overwork.

- Context: Chaplains need to be aware of burnout signs in themselves and others and take steps to prevent it.

14. Self-Care

- Definition: Activities and practices that individuals engage in to maintain their health and well-being.

- Context: Self-care is essential for chaplains to sustain their ability to support others effectively.

15. Cultural Sensitivity

- Definition: Awareness and respect for the cultural differences and diversity of individuals.

- Context: Chaplains practice cultural sensitivity to provide respectful and effective care in diverse workplaces.

16. Empathy

- Definition: The ability to understand and share the feelings of another person.

- Context: Empathy is a crucial skill for chaplains in providing compassionate support.

17. Referral

- Definition: The process of directing an individual to another professional or service for additional support.

- Context: Chaplains may refer employees to mental health professionals, medical providers, or other resources.

18. Holistic Care

- Definition: An approach to care that addresses the physical, emotional, mental, and spiritual needs of individuals.

- Context: Corporate chaplains provide holistic care to support the overall well-being of employees.

19. Resilience

- Definition: The ability to recover from setbacks, adapt to change, and keep going in the face of adversity.

- Context: Chaplains help build resilience in employees by providing support and coping strategies.

20. Active Listening

- Definition: A communication technique that involves fully concentrating, understanding, responding, and remembering what the other person is saying.

- Context: Active listening is a fundamental skill for chaplains to understand and support employees effectively.

21. Chaplaincy Supervision

- Definition: Regular meetings between chaplains and their supervisors to review their work, provide feedback, and offer support.

- Context: Supervision helps chaplains maintain professional standards and address any challenges they encounter.

22. Vocational Counseling

- Definition: Guidance and support provided to individuals regarding their career and vocational choices.

- Context: Corporate chaplains may offer vocational counseling to help employees navigate career decisions and changes.

23. Bereavement Support

- Definition: Assistance provided to individuals who are grieving the loss of a loved one.

- Context: Chaplains offer bereavement support to employees coping with loss, helping them navigate their grief.

24. Conflict Resolution

- Definition: The process of resolving disputes or disagreements between individuals or groups.

- Context: Chaplains may facilitate conflict resolution to promote a harmonious workplace environment.

Conclusion

This glossary of terms provides a foundational understanding of key concepts and terminology used in corporate chaplaincy. Familiarity with these terms enhances the ability of chaplains to communicate effectively, maintain professional standards, and provide high-quality care to employees. As the field of chaplaincy continues to evolve, staying updated with these terms and their applications is essential for ongoing professional development.

Dr. Maxwell Shimba

A GLITTERING OBSESSION

Appendix: Resources for Corporate Chaplains

References

Introduction

A comprehensive list of sources and further reading materials is essential for corporate chaplains seeking to deepen their understanding and enhance their practice. The following references include books, articles, journals, and websites that provide valuable insights into chaplaincy, pastoral care, and spiritual support in the workplace.

Books

1. Doehring, Carrie. The Practice of Pastoral Care: A Postmodern Approach. Westminster John Knox Press, 2015.

2. Roberts, Stephen B., ed. Professional Spiritual & Pastoral Care: A Practical Clergy and Chaplain's Handbook. Skylight Paths Publishing, 2011.

3. Fitchett, George, and Steve Nolan, eds. Spiritual Care in Practice: Case Studies in Healthcare Chaplaincy. Jessica Kingsley Publishers, 2015.

4. Nouwen, Henri J.M. The Wounded Healer: Ministry in Contemporary Society. Image Books, 1979.

5. Sullivan, Winnifred Fallers. A Ministry of Presence: Chaplaincy, Spiritual Care, and the Law. University of Chicago Press, 2014.

6. Koenig, Harold G. Soul Care: Christian Faith and Academic Administration. Oxford University Press, 2011.

7. Denney, Jeanne. The Art of Listening in the Healing Process. CreateSpace Independent Publishing Platform, 2015.

Journals and Articles

1. Journal of Pastoral Care & Counseling (JPCC).

- Website: [jpccjournal.com](https://www.jpccjournal.com)

2. Journal of Health Care Chaplaincy.

- Website: [tandfonline.com/loi/whcc20](https://www.tandfonline.com/loi/whcc20)

3. The Journal of Pastoral Psychology.

- Website: [springer.com/journal/11089](https://www.springer.com/journal/11089)

4. Health and Social Care Chaplaincy.

- Website: [equinoxpub.com/journals/index.php/HSCC](https://www .equinoxpub.com/journals/index.php/HSCC)

Professional Organizations

1. Association of Professional Chaplains (APC).

- Website: [www.professionalchaplains.org](https://www.professionalc haplains.org)

2. National Association of Catholic Chaplains (NACC).

- Website: www.nacc.org

3. National Association of Jewish Chaplains (NAJC).

- Website: www.najc.org

4. Spiritual Care Association (SCA).

- Website: [www.spiritualcareassociation.org](https://www.spiritualcare association.org)

5. College of Pastoral Supervision and Psychotherapy (CPSP).

- Website: www.cpsp.org

6. Healthcare Chaplains Ministry Association (HCMA).

-   Website: www.healthcarechaplains.org

7. Military Chaplains Association (MCA).

- Website: www.mca-usa.org

8. American Association of Pastoral Counselors (AAPC).

- Website: www.aapc.org

Online Resources and Learning Platforms

1. Chaplaincy Innovation Lab.

-   Website: www.chaplaincyinnovation.org

2. Spiritual Care Association Learning Center.

-   Website: www.spiritualcareassociation.org/learning-center.html

3. Coursera.

-   Website: www.coursera.org

4. edX.

- Website: www.edx.org

5. LinkedIn Learning.

- Website: www.linkedin.com/learning

Research Databases

1. PubMed.

- Website: www.pubmed.gov

2. JSTOR.

- Website: www.jstor.org

3. Google Scholar.

- Website: scholar.google.com

4. PsycINFO.

- Access through institutional subscriptions.

Conclusion

These references provide a solid foundation for corporate chaplains seeking to enhance their knowledge, skills, and professional development. Engaging with these materials and organizations will help chaplains stay informed about the latest research and best practices, ensuring they provide high-quality, evidence-based care to employees. Continuous learning and professional growth are essential for maintaining excellence in chaplaincy, and these resources offer valuable support in achieving that goal.

Dr. Maxwell Shimba

CONCLUSION

THE FUTURE OF CORPORATE CHAPLAINCY

Emerging Trends and Challenges

As the workplace continues to evolve, the field of corporate chaplaincy is also experiencing significant changes. Several emerging trends and challenges are shaping the future of this vital profession:

1. Integration of Technology

- Trend: The use of technology in chaplaincy is expanding, with virtual counseling sessions, online support groups, and digital resources becoming more common.

- Challenge: Maintaining personal connections and ensuring confidentiality in a digital environment.

2. Focus on Diversity and Inclusion

- Trend: There is an increasing emphasis on diversity and inclusion within the workplace, requiring chaplains to be culturally competent and sensitive to the needs of a diverse workforce.

- Challenge: Providing spiritual care that respects and honors the wide range of beliefs and cultural backgrounds of employees.

3. Mental Health Awareness

- Trend: Growing awareness of mental health issues has led to a greater demand for chaplaincy services that address emotional and psychological well-being.

- Challenge: Ensuring chaplains are adequately trained in mental health support and can effectively collaborate with mental health professionals.

4. Work-Life Balance

- Trend: The importance of work-life balance is increasingly recognized, and chaplains play a crucial role in supporting employees in achieving this balance.

- Challenge: Helping employees navigate the boundary between work and personal life in an era of remote and hybrid work models.

5. Sustainability and Social Responsibility

- Trend: Companies are focusing more on sustainability and social responsibility, and chaplains can support these initiatives by promoting ethical behavior and a sense of purpose.

- Challenge: Integrating spiritual care with corporate social responsibility efforts in a meaningful way.

The Evolving Role of Spirituality in the Workplace

The role of spirituality in the workplace is evolving, with a growing recognition of its importance for overall well-being and organizational success:

1. Holistic Well-Being

- Evolving Role: Spirituality is increasingly seen as a crucial component of holistic well-being, contributing to physical, emotional, and mental health.

- Impact: Employees who feel spiritually supported are more likely to experience greater job satisfaction, resilience, and overall well-being.

2. Ethical Decision-Making

- Evolving Role: Spirituality can guide ethical decision-making and promote a values-based corporate culture.

- Impact: Organizations that incorporate spiritual principles into their operations are more likely to foster trust, integrity, and ethical behavior among employees.

3. Community and Connection

- Evolving Role: Spirituality fosters a sense of community and connection among employees, creating a supportive and inclusive work environment.

- Impact: Strong community bonds within the workplace can enhance teamwork, collaboration, and a sense of belonging.

4. Purpose and Meaning

- Evolving Role: Spirituality helps employees find purpose and meaning in their work, aligning personal values with organizational goals.

- Impact: Employees who find meaning in their work are more motivated, engaged, and committed to their organization's mission.

The Ongoing Impact of Chaplaincy on Corporate Culture

Corporate chaplaincy continues to have a profound impact on corporate culture, shaping the way organizations approach employee well-being and organizational success:

1. Enhancing Employee Well-Being

- Impact: Chaplaincy services address the holistic needs of employees, supporting their physical, emotional, mental, and spiritual health.

- Result: Improved employee well-being leads to increased job satisfaction, productivity, and retention.

2. Promoting a Positive Work Environment

- Impact: Chaplains contribute to a positive and supportive work environment by fostering trust, compassion, and empathy.

- Result: A positive work environment enhances employee morale, reduces stress, and promotes a culture of respect and collaboration.

3. Supporting Organizational Change

- Impact: Chaplains help employees navigate organizational changes and transitions, providing support and stability during periods of uncertainty.

- Result: Effective support during change can reduce anxiety, increase resilience, and facilitate smoother transitions.

4. Strengthening Organizational Values

- Impact: Chaplains reinforce organizational values and ethical standards, helping to create a culture of integrity and accountability.

- Result: A strong values-based culture enhances the organization's reputation, attracts top talent, and fosters long-term success.

Conclusion

The future of corporate chaplaincy is bright, with emerging trends and evolving roles highlighting the importance of spiritual care in the workplace. As organizations continue to recognize the value of holistic employee support, the role of chaplains will become even more integral to fostering a positive and inclusive corporate culture. By staying attuned to emerging trends, embracing the evolving role of spirituality, and addressing the ongoing impact of their work, corporate chaplains can continue to make a significant difference in the lives of employees and the success of organizations.

Corporate chaplaincy is not just about providing support during times of crisis; it is about nurturing a culture of care, compassion, and ethical integrity that benefits both employees and the organization as a whole. As we look to the future, the commitment to continuous learning, professional development, and staying connected with the latest research and practices will ensure that chaplains remain effective, resilient, and impactful in their roles.

Dr. Maxwell Shimba